THE ROMANCE OF ESSEX INNS

THE ROMANCE OF
ESSEX INNS
by

GLYN MORGAN

IAN HENRY PUBLICATIONS
1983

First published by Letchworth Printers Ltd., 1964
Second edition, with new illustrations, 1983

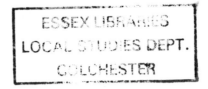

ISBN 0 86025 872 6

Printed and bound in Great Britain by
The Garden City Press Limited
Letchworth, Hertfordshire SG6 1JS
for Ian Henry Publications, Ltd.
38 Parkstone Avenue, Hornchurch, Essex RM11 3LW

CONTENTS

PAGE

FOREWORD 7

I. THE WORLD'S AN INN 11

II. MADMAN AND MARTYR 19

III. HE THAT BUYS ALE BUYS NOTHING ELSE 22

IV. MANIE FAYRE INNES 26

V. CHARMS OF AN INN 33

VI. COLCHESTER 37

VII. THROUGH DEDHAM VALE 42

VIII. BACK OF THE BEYOND 49

IX. MEHALAH COUNTRY 57

X. BRADWELL AND BURNHAM 65

XI. REVENUE LAWS AND OFFICERS FOR EVER 69

XII. INNS OF THE SEA REACH 78

XIII. REVOLTING INCIDENTS 84

XIV. EAST TILBURY TO CHELMSFORD 89

XV. TILBURY FORT TO BRENTWOOD 96

XVI. IN THE PATH OF THE PILGRIMS 101

XVII. GRAYS TO RAINHAM 111

XVIII. LONDON'S RIVER 116

XIX. INNS OF THE FOREST 121

XX. DUNMOW TO BRENTWOOD 137

XXI. BRAINTREE TO COGGESHALL 145

XXII. THROUGH THE HOP-LANDS 150

XXIII. INN SIGNS OF ESSEX 161

FOREWORD

The inns mentioned in this book are those that have given me pleasure on account of their history, their architecture or simply because of the good company I have enjoyed in them. I have tried to be as accurate as possible, but this is difficult when the subjects are for ever changing in appearance due to the efforts of the brewers or disappearing entirely due to the efforts of speculative builders.

The writer about inns is a thwarted man. He spends days searching for documents that, when found, provide little information of interest to the general reader. Unlike churches, very few inns have recorded histories. In some cases the brewers have been helpful, but I was astonished to learn that one firm had actually lost its records! The final typescript version of this book suffered a similar fate when in the hands of a local printer. The loss caused difficulties and delays and made the task of Letchworth Printers Ltd. much more difficult. I wish to thank them for their patience and help and also for allowing me to reprint the first six chapters of this book, which appeared originally in their admirable magazine *Essex Countryside*.

Thanks must also be given to all landlords who made my researches a pleasure; to Mr. Stansfield, of the Ind Coope brewery, Romford, for technical help on brewing; to authors who so readily allowed me to quote from their works; to Mrs. R. Burton for help in preparing the typescript; and to Mr. F. G. Dove for patiently correcting the proofs.

I must also thank all those who have sent me information. This has been most welcome, but I am still eager for more, since every scrap helps to fill up the enormous gaps in our knowledge of Essex inns.

A NOTE ON THIS EDITION

Since this book first appeared some twenty years ago the face of Essex has undergone considerable changes. Great roads have been built cutting giant swathes through the countryside; the hearts of many towns have been gutted to be replaced by shopping precincts of varying merit; urban one-way systems have been introduced which frequently confuse the visiting motorist without ensuring a safer life for the pedestrian; and new towns have been built. To allow all these changes to take place a number of inns had to be demolished or converted to other uses. Despite all the changes, however, I decided against rewriting the book since most of the inns mentioned in it are, happily, still with us and to have omitted those that have disappeared would have affected the continuity of the narrative. This decision, as well as the topographical changes, might make it a little more difficult for the reader intent on field work but I feel sure that the search will, none the less, prove enjoyable and rewarding.

The character of most inns has changed over the last two decades, usually for the better. Brewers have gone to great pains to make the signs of their houses more attractive; catering has reached a higher standard and the décor and comfort of the bars have improved considerably. It could be argued that the interiors of some establishments are scarcely in keeping with the immediate neighbourhood. Sometimes it comes as a shock to enter a simple country pub with its plain façade to find an interior as plush as that of a West End lounge. One is reminded of the Doctor Who fantasy where the very ordinary police box conceals a technological wonderland.

Not all the innovations have been universally welcomed. The replacement of landlords by managers in a number of pubs has been criticised on the grounds that managers lack the incentive to provide the very best service for the customers, although this has been strongly denied. But who would deny that the introduction of one-armed bandits, juke-boxes and space invaders has made the attainment of a quiet drink and a chat an almost impossible goal.

Sadly I have to record the names of those pubs that no longer exist as such. The Epping Forest area has lost a number. Two well-known landmarks have ceased to cater for the thirsty traveller —the Wake Arms at the time of writing being but an empty shell and Turpin's Cave a private house. The Cock in Waltham Abbey has crowed its last, while a small menagerie—a White Hart, a Swan and a White Lion—has deserted Epping Town. Another White Hart, in Great Bardfield, is showing signs of its great age and, without a keeper will decay rapidly. A great loss to Saffron Walden and to the County was the destruction by fire of the celebrated Rose and Crown. Equally sad was the demolition of the fine old Bell in Upminster to make way for shops of decidely inferior architectural merit. Despite its disappearance its name is still preserved in the corner where it once stood just as the estate on the fringe of Ingatestone perpetuates that of the former Chase Hotel. A frequent victim of the chase, a White Hart, has gone from Horndon-on-the-Hill and the King's Head in nearby Stanford-le-Hope has been converted into a wine bar, although it still retains its old name. Some other inns still clinging to their former names despite their change of function are The Star in Great Dunmow and the Cock in High Easter. They are now restaurants, as is also the old Three Horseshoes in High Ongar whose present sign displays, not the shoes of an animal, but those of a human. They are carved attractively out of wood.

Of the east coast hostelries mentioned in this book three have ceased to function as inns—the Wave in Heybridge, the Three Crowns in Rowhedge and the ancient Falcon in Wivenhoe, all having been converted into private residences. Gone, too, is the ferry that once operated between these last towns, but fortunately the view of the Wivenhoe river front as seen from west bank of the Stour remains unaltered. Surely this must be one of the most attractive views in Essex.

The river front in West Mersea can make no such claim and its recent transformation in order to accommodate the growing number of sailing enthusiasts has done little to enhance the view.

Some of the older features have been swept away to make way for the more modern constructions, so the visitor will look in vain for that link with the town's shady past—the old smuggler's lookout.

Many of the drawings have been specially made for this edition, but I have purposely retained some of the original illustrations so that the reader can compare some of the present buildings with their appearance of twenty years ago.

UPMINSTER, May, 1983

CHAPTER I

THE WORLD'S AN INN

IT was not so long ago that the cry of the Welsh drovers—
" Haiptrw! "—rang loud and clear along the Essex roads
and over the Ilford fields. Farmers, hearing the warning,
mustered their cattle to avoid being swept along in the maelstrom,
and the whips of the London-bound coaches reined in their
horses to avoid causing a stampede.

All this rural bustle has been replaced by less pleasant sounds,
and there is but little to remind us in Essex of the age-old traffic
save a lone gravestone or a strange Welsh name in some parish
register. But for centuries the drovers had come from far-off Wales
to help feed the ever-growing population of London. After the long
journey the sheep, the cows and the geese were too lean for the
London tables, so a period of fattening in Essex, the " English
Goshen," was necessary.

One of the favourite haunts of the drovers was the Three Rabbits,
a modern version of which still stands near Manor Park station.
It was in the old inn that the Welshmen enjoyed a pint of " cwrw,"
swapped tales that lost nothing in the telling, clinched many a
financial deal and filled the air with some lilting harmony of the
homeland.

The advent of speedy transport killed the drovers' trade—a
trade that can be traced back for centuries. Medieval toll charges
for the Wye bridge at Hereford and for the Mountford bridge at
Shrewsbury are still in existence. By the eighteenth century the
comparative trickle of those far-off days had swollen to a tremendous flood.

Through Herefordshire alone 30,000 head of black cattle passed
eastwards from the summer and autumn fairs of Wales. However,
by the end of the eighteenth century the " Haiptrw ho! " of the
drovers had given way to the sound of the postilion's horn, and

no longer did the Welsh sing-song clash with the clipped speech of Essex. By this time the road from Harwich to London had grown in importance and the accents heard in the Three Rabbits were many and varied—and seldom Welsh. Not that the inn was a noted coaching house. According to Thomas Hood only one post-chaise a day left the inn for the short journey to Wanstead.

The postilion of this service appears in one of Hood's novels, *Tylney Hall*, published in 1834. He was a character of Dickensian mould, with a remarkable propensity for landing objects, animate and inanimate, in trouble. Lucky were the passengers whose chaise did not end up in a ditch!

Haiptrw ho!—and away we go along the Essex Great Road that leads to Harwich! The Red Lion and the Angel in Ilford are both old coaching houses, now but shadows of what they were when coaches ran at half-hour intervals through the small village that was Ilford.

The road to Romford has no claim to beauty, but as we travel along it we do at least feel that the character of the great city is changing. We feel that we are approaching the countryside, and this impression is heightened when we enter Romford itself, with its wide market place, teeming with thousands now where formerly gawked a few hundred from the neighbouring villages.

John Taylor, the Water Poet, wrote in 1636 that Romford had " a sweet, savery, clean and gainful market for hogs and all sorts of swine, and what else is needful to man's life." He did not mention that the town was granted its charter to hold the market by Henry III in 1247.

This John Taylor was a " character." He was born in Gloucester in 1580, but lived most of his life in London. It was from his apprenticeship to a London waterman that he derived his pseudonym of the Water Poet. Pressed into the Navy, he sailed under the Earl of Essex and was later to boast of his service to Elizabeth. When he was discharged he again became a waterman, but by the middle of the reign of James I he was complaining that his trade had deteriorated considerably because of the increase in the number of watermen, the increase in the number of coaches and the removal of the theatres from the Surrey side of the river. It was now that he turned to rhyme. His facility in composing witty verses on topical events helped him to supplement his waterman's wages. He also hit upon a scheme which can be recommended to all those who contemplate writing a guide book. He planned a journey, circularized all those who he thought would be interested, including the landlords of inns *en route*, then, when he considered that the tour could be made without financial loss to himself, he set off.

Inns where he met with satisfactory hospitality were commended in the subsequent account of his journey, but unfriendly inns met with the castigation they deserved. Such treatment nowadays would be followed by a libel action—more's the pity! Although the accounts of these journeys are of no great literary merit, they do provide us with useful information about the inns of those days.

The success of his journeys in the vicinity of London encouraged Taylor to go farther afield. Between 1613 and about 1622 he travelled to Scotland, York and Salisbury, and described each journey in a book.

Because of the Plague he went in 1625 to Oxford, where he devoted himself to serious study. He returned to the same town seventeen years later, this time becoming landlord of an inn. He combined the profession with the writing of scurrilous lampoons against the Parliamentarians. Charles showed his appreciation of his services by making him a Yeoman of the Guard.

At the surrender of Oxford in 1645, Taylor returned to London, where he became landlord of the Crown in Hanover Street, Long Acre. After the execution of the king he changed the sign to the Mourning Crown. Not unnaturally, the powers considered this demonstration to be " malignant," so Taylor substituted his own head on the sign and changed the name to the Poet's Head, adding the inscription :

> " There's many a head stands for a sign,
>
> Then, gentle reader, why not mine? "

On the other side was the couplet :

> " Though I deserve not, I desire
>
> The laurel wreath, the poet's hire."

He made no attempt to conceal his political sympathies, so it is not surprising that a warrant was issued for his arrest in August 1649. He was not arrested, however, but continued to live in his inn until his death in 1653 and was buried at St. Martin's-in-the-Fields.

Taylor mentioned that Romford had four taverns—the Angel, the Bell, the White Hart and the Cocke. Only the White Hart now remains. In stage-coach days it was an important hostelry and all day long coaches left on their journeys in every direction. It was at the White Hart that the soldiers escorting the body of Queen Caroline back to Brunswick stopped for refreshments—meanwhile leaving the body outside! It is a sad story, the sadness dimming but little over the years.

Caroline's was a marriage of convenience. There was no love. George, Prince of Wales, was heavily in debt, but Parliament would not provide the much-needed money until the heir to the throne took a wife. Caroline was the unhappy victim.

George seemed determined not to show the slightest affection for his wife. Even on the wedding day the seventeen-year-old girl was insulted and George's behaviour scarcely concealed the fact that she was unwelcome. Such a marriage could not last long. In 1820 the king's ministers brought the matter to a climax by instituting divorce proceedings in order to please their royal master at the time of his succession. Popular feeling, however, was against the king, and the Bill of Pains and Penalties was withdrawn before reaching the Commons.

The death of Caroline shortly afterwards released her from her unhappy environment, but even in death George was determined to humiliate her. Her body was to be taken back to her own land along the road that we are now following. The king ordered that the body should not be taken through the city—but he reckoned without the people. They were determined that it should go through and forced it the way they wanted by barricading the side streets. Even the shots fired by the soldiers had little effect.

The cortège proceeded to Romford on that hot summer's day, arriving outside the White Hart about 8.30 in the evening. Many of the followers wanted to remain overnight in the town, but the king's orders were quite definite—to proceed to Chelmsford and rest the coffin in the church until the following day.

So at eleven o'clock the procession started once more. It was a spectacular and moving sight. With blazing torches the chief citizens of Romford led the way out of the town, and some miles beyond, their homage paid, they lined the road and, as the dead queen passed, extinguished the flaming brands one by one.

Late that night the coffin was placed in Chelmsford church. By eleven o'clock of the following morning the procession was once more under way. At Colchester it paused again while the corpse lay in St. Peter's church. The undertaker insisted that the king's orders were to proceed, without pause, to Harwich. Little wonder, then, that this king's man removed the plaque that sympathizers had placed on the coffin, for inscribed on it were the words: "Deposited, Caroline of Brunswick, the injured Queen of England." Harwich was reached the next day, and soon the body was returned to Brunswick and laid to rest in the cathedral.

Of the other inns mentioned by John Taylor, the Angel was probably the oldest. We can trace it back to the days of Henry VIII, although at that time it was known as the Bull. In a document of 1664 drawn up by Francis Pointeau, a lawyer of Anjou, we learn that Robert Rich, Knight, Baron of Kensington, at that time living in Anjou, " acknowledging the merits, good and grateful services of Benedict Barber, his follower and servant, gave unto him by a donation irrevocable amongst living men one house, with the appurtenances and dependencies thereof sitted and situated in the towne of Romford in the province or countye of Essex, in England, the which house is an Ine whereatt hangeth a signe the picture of an Angell, with the garden, lands and orchards belonging unto the said house which is adjoining to the bridge of the said towne of Romford."

The Angel ceased to exist—if angels can!—about the year 1772.

Church House, Romford, is a well-known feature of the ancient market place. It was built by Avery Cornburgh in 1486 as a chantry for the church of Edward the Confessor. Henry VIII seized the property and it then became the Cock and Bell inn. Centuries later, in 1908 to be exact, it reverted to the Church, thanks to the efforts of the then vicar of Romford, Dr. Whitcombe.

We must not pass through Romford without meeting one of its famous sons—Francis Quarles, born in 1592. He was a family man, equally fertile in this rôle—eighteen children!—as he was as a versifier. That he knew the Angel and the White Hart we can hardly doubt. It is pleasant to think that he had them in mind when he composed those lines by which he is best remembered:

> " The world's an Inne; and I her guest,
> I eate, I drinke, I take my reste;
> My Hostesse, Nature, doth deny me
> Nothing, wherewith she can supply me;
> Where having stay'd awhile, I pay
> Her lavish Bills, and goe my way."

Certainly the building in Hare Street that is now the Ship inn was standing in his day, and standing then as now on beaten earth, for it has no footings. The slap-happy way in which it was erected would appal the modern building inspector, and no doubt he would have condemned it as unfit for living in because of its insecure foundations! But there it still is and will be 500 years hence.

It was in 1950 that the true character of the building was revealed when the weatherboarding was stripped from the outside and the plasterboard from the inside. True, the delightful Elizabethan brick chimney was visible, but the extent of the Elizabethan work was not generally recognized. Nowadays it is there for all to see. The chimney still looks as if it is about to topple over, the tiled roof is varied and rich in colour, and the timbering of the façade looks as if it were erected by a drunken man. Inside there is little decoration, the simplicity of the furnishing not detracting in any way from the genuine Elizabethan fireplaces and the old oak beams.

In the public bar hangs a small plaque decorated with the date 1798 and the smiling face of the sun resplendent. Originally this plaque was affixed to the exterior wall and indicated that the old Ship was insured by the Sun Insurance Company. Fire insurance companies only came into being some time after the Great Fire of London when one Nicholas Barban pioneered the idea. For thirteen years he worked alone, but enlarged his enterprise in 1680 by inviting other business men to join him. The success of Barban's companies prompted others to form rival companies, with names like the Sun, the Phœnix and the Lion. Some modern companies are also known by their signs, but there the similarity between the tiny pioneers and the modern giants ends. One other old-time object preserved in the Ship is a curling iron, a relic of the old curling rink which stood behind the inn.

Ale seems to be the most appropriate drink in this building erected in the reign of the first Elizabeth, but in the Squirrel's Head, not half a mile away along the Balgores Lane, a martini, a sherry or some such aperitif seems more suitable, for in this ultra-modern inn, which arose out of the ashes of the old bombed weatherboarded predecessor, an attempt has been made to blend the originality of decor of the reign of the second Elizabeth with the traditional features of the English pub.

Our way leads to Brentwood. At the foot of the long hill into

THE VIPER
FRYERNING

SPREAD EAGLE
· WITHAM ·

The RED LION
COLCHESTER

this town is a group of buildings consisting of the **Kit Kat Café**, the Moat House and the Golden Fleece—a group not to be passed by in a hurry.

The inn is said to stand on the site of the twelfth-century priory of St. Peter, but no greater age than 500 years is claimed for the inn itself. Upstairs, the fine oak beams in the Nelson room give proof of the age, but the proof that the admiral used the room on his journeys to and from Harwich is not forthcoming. Hay-carters used the inn a great deal. On the down journey they placed their meals in a long oven which was then locked with a strong padlock, since the other hay-carters were not to be trusted ! On the return journey the landlord was paid one halfpenny for the use of the oven and the carter then ate his warm meal. The oven has long since been removed, but the shining copper measures hanging from a beam still link us with those days. When spirits were brought round the inns in great barrels, the desired quantity was siphoned into these copper jugs belonging to the inn.

Perhaps the most curious object among the many to be found in this warm, cosy bar is the yard-of-ale glass. John Evelyn mentions this type of measure when, on February 11, 1685, he attended the proclamation of the king at Bromley " when the High Sheriff read the titles and, after many shouts of the people, His Majesty's health being drunk in a flute glass of a yard long, by the Sheriff, Commande Officers, and Chiefe Gentleman." According to Dillon, an authority on glass, the yard-glass was an exaggerated development of the Venetian or Dutch *flute* glasses—long, slender drinking vessels.

From various records it appears that the yard-glass was used chiefly at initiation ceremonies. To gain entrance to the council chamber at the ancient Hemley Venison Feast the initiate had to drink a yard of ale. At Eton too in the last century aspirants to the Cellar had to quaff the yard of ale in order to obtain full membership.

Thirst alone was not sufficient guarantee that the two pints of ale in the glass could be drunk. The vessel seems designed to thwart one's best intentions. It is a yard-long tube, swollen into a large bulb at the base and opening like a funnel at the other end. While drinking from it the initiate has to control the angle in order to regulate the flow of liquid and to permit a steady entry of air. Much practice is essential, for if too much air enters the bulb it

causes a sudden surge of liquid which proves disastrous to the
drinker. So anyone capable of drinking the two pints from the
yard glass was without doubt a person worthy to become a member
of any society; indeed, even to drink " a double glass o' the
inwariable " from a normal-shaped tankard without removing
the lips is quite a feat!

Before proceeding to Brentwood proper it is worth while taking
the first turning left beyond the Golden Fleece to South Weald.
Opposite the church is Tower Arms, a name derived not from the
fact that the tower of that church dominates the view seen through
the front windows of the inn, but from the name of former owners
of Weald Park.

The early-eighteenth-century Tower Arms is substantially built
of red and blue bricks. The interior is more homely in a slightly
Victorian way. Glass cases containing stuffed specimens of local
fauna, prints (amusing and serious, good, bad and indifferent),
foxes' heads and brushes and divers knick-knacks bedeck the
walls and divert the patron. On the other hand, the framed copy
of Kipling's " If " can be stimulating at a certain point of intoxi-
cation! Equally stimulating is a walk in the extensive park that
expands behind the church.

GOLDEN FLEECE   BROOK STREET

LION & LAMB · BRENTWOOD

CHAPTER II

MADMAN AND MARTYR

IN 1221 the abbot of St. Osyth built a chapel in Brentwood
and dedicated it to St. Thomas the Martyr. Little is now left
of this ancient structure, and the few remaining fragments are
seldom noticed by the fans hurrying to the super cinema or by the
shoppers in the High Street, but for centuries this small chapel
was the focal point of pilgrims from far and wide on their way to
Canterbury.

Before the establishment of inns in the fourteenth century most
pilgrims were accommodated by the ecclesiastical authorities.
Later, when the inns were built, some pilgrims sought shelter
beneath their roofs. It is not unlikely that the ancient Crown inn
was a pilgrim hostel. There is still a Crown Street, but the inn is
only a memory now. John Taylor mentioned it in 1616, and even
the more sedate Morant, in 1768, noted its existence: " Very
ancient, as appears from buildings at the back of it. Mr. Symonds
in his Collections saith, he was informed from the master, who had
writings in his custody to show it, that it had been an Inn three
hundred years; that there had been eighty-one owners, amongst
which an Earl of Oxford and an Earl of Sussex."

In the eighteenth century the Crown was a coaching house of
some importance, since Brentwood stood at the junction of roads
from London to Harwich and from the Rochford to the Barstable
hundred. Towards the end of the century the cost of travel increased
so that the landlord of the Crown announced that he and certain other
landlords had decided to let post horses at the " old rates—a shilling
a mile for a pair, 1s. 9d. for four horses; and fourpence halfpenny
for a single horse and oats at threepence a quartern as heretofore."

Two years later, in May 1796, a shot broke the stillness of the
early morning as a private chariot pulled up at the Crown. In those
days loiterers were often encouraged to move faster by the firing

of arms, so the postilion can be excused for ignoring the shot. Later the journey was resumed, and at the Angel, Ilford, horses, driver and postilion were all changed.

When the chariot was approaching the Globe, Mile End, another shot rang out. This time the perceptive postilion realized that the shot was fired in his chariot. As if to confirm his conclusion, a gun was thrown through the window. But our man was undisturbed! He took no action. Even the rather alarming behaviour of his passengers failed to ruffle his calm.

Arriving at Argyle Street, the postilion got down to ask his passengers their destination. " The Bishop of Norwich " came the reply. This was too much even for him, so he repeated the question. This time the passenger did not reply but started pummelling the poor postilion, leaving off only so that he could remove his clothes. This crazy behaviour and the sight of the dead body in the chariot convinced the postilion that all was not well! With the help of some passers-by he seized the madman and hauled him to the lockup.

The tale that subsequently unfolded was in keeping with these strange events.

Sir Edmund Lucan revealed that the dead man was Lord Charles Townsend and the other his brother Frederick, sons of the Marquis of Townsend. Sir Edmund and the brother had gone to Great Yarmouth to celebrate the marquis's victory in the recent election. The brothers had been on the best of terms, but had " joined in the festivities too much." Their behaviour became so strange that Sir Edmund decided to follow them back to London.

What had happened in the carriage? According to Lord Frederick they had been discussing a religious subject when his brother placed a pistol in his mouth and killed himself. So upset was Frederick at this incident that he too attempted suicide, but the pistol failed to act.

Medical evidence supported him. Absence of scars on the mouth of Lord Charles indicated that no force had been used to insert the large pistol. Evidently, too, Sir Frederick was far from normal mentally. The verdict—" the deceased had been killed by a pistol-ball, but from whose hand unknown."

Death enters into our next tale, too, but death untouched by madmen, death that shines forth like a clear light.

For three days—Saturday, Sunday and Monday of the month of August in the year 1555—William Hunter, a boy of nineteen, was detained in the Swan inn. He was not a native of Brentwood, but had moved to the town from London with his father. Finding a Bible, he taught himself to read it. This " meddling with the Scriptures " was, in the opinion of Bishop Bonner, a crime, and in due course William was taken before the bishop. He was not unmoved by the youthfulness of the " meddler "; indeed, he offered William the freedom of the city and a grant to set himself up in business, on certain conditions.

" I thank you for your great offer; notwithstanding, my Lord, I cannot find in my heart to turn from God for the love of the world."

There could be but one sequel to such a brave reply, and William was returned to the Swan to await his fate. A letter from the queen offered his life if he would recant, but his reply was as before. On the stake he was bound in chains. As the flames rose around him he shouted: " Son of God shine upon me." Strangely the sun did shine, and all who watched marvelled.

Sir Antony Browne, the man who ordered the burning, founded Brentwood Grammar School for Boys, to teach " learning, virtue and manners " !

The ancient Crown was pulled down in the first half of the nineteenth century, but another inn of great age still stands in the High Street—the White Hart. Step from the bustle of the main street through the old coachway and you step from the twentieth to the fifteenth century. True, many alterations have been carried out, but the fifteenth-century gallery still surrounds the yard. Not many of our present inns can claim continuous service from Shakespeare's day, but the White Hart was built as an inn and there seems little likelihood of its being anything else for many years to come. Mention of Shakespeare reminds us that many of his plays were performed in inn-yards, and it is well known that the design of playhouses, or theatres as we now call them, was strongly influenced by the galleried inn-yard.

In the coaching era, the White Hart was a well-known hostelry and horses could be changed at this point. As early as 1764 the coach which ran from the Black Bull, Bishopsgate, to the Great White Horse, Ipswich, called here on its run—a run, incidentally, which took only ten hours to complete. At a later date the landlord, Richard Wicks, was sufficiently enterprising to run his own service to London at eight o'clock in the morning, to return at 6.30 the same evening.

CHAPTER III

HE THAT BUYS ALE BUYS NOTHING ELSE

THE road beyond Brentwood sways and curves like a gentle switchback. Here and there is the modern version of the eighteenth-century hostel—the pull-in. One could almost write " pull-inn," since these establishments have replaced to some extent the function of their predecessors. Here you can eat, generally well, but without such refinements as tablecloths. The helpings are generous and the tea is strong and hot. Prices are reasonable. Lorry drivers are the principal patrons of these " caffs " as they are familiarly called, but schoolboys on cycles and motorists are not unknown as customers, although they may call them " cafés " or even " cayffs."

Pull-in nomenclature is unimaginative. True there is an intimacy, a friendliness, about Bob's or Pete's or Joe's, but it would be a bold artist who would attempt to paint a sign with such prosaic material. Not that all the pull-ins deserve signs. The standard of architecture is far lower than it ever was in the case of inns. We are all too well acquainted with dilapidated shacks desecrating many a beauty spot, and we are inclined to condemn all pull-ins for that reason. That they serve a useful need no one doubts, but would that as much serious thought was put into their design as is put into inn-planning, for then the countryside would be much the richer.

Why is there no such thing as an ugly windmill? The 300-year-old post mill at Mountnessing is no exception. Soon we note the George and Dragon, with its rich red roof, and the Prince of Wales, commanding a fine view of the mill.

Before entering Ingatestone village a cut-out sign of two stiff yet athletic-looking deer proclaims the proximity of the unique hotel of the Essex Great Road—the Chase. Here you can eat a good meal, play a game of squash, badminton or golf, go horse-riding. Until recently there was also a fine swimming pool.

The inn is appropriately named, since the territories of three well-known Essex hunts meet nearby. So do not be surprised to see a pheasant, a wild duck or even a fox somewhere in the eighteen acres of grounds. Completely in keeping with the inn are the hunting murals adorning the ballroom.

Until comparatively recently the Crown inn marked the western limits of Ingatestone village. In 1472 John Wynch not only kept the inn but also worked as a mason. Was it from too much work that he died that year? We do not know, but we do know that his widow continued to live in the inn, since it is recorded that she charged excess for her home-brewed ale, and for the bread which she also made. For these crimes she was fined 3d. She was in good company, however, for the constable, William Benton, who was also the fishmonger, and William Chapman, the woodward, who had to account for all the timber of the manor, were also fined at the same time.

Dropping down into Ingatestone, one is aware of the massive church tower looming dark and sullen over the old coaching town. The Spread Eagle still proclaims its past, for " Commercial Inn and Posting House " is writ large on the façade, and although the Bell makes no such claim a mere glance is sufficient to establish its lineage. One cannot help wondering how the coaches managed to turn into the yard, for the street is narrow here and it was a matter of pride with the old whips to turn into the inn-yard from the king's highway with scarcely a slackening of speed.

The inn displays the sign of a bell with the age-old invocation: *Vivos voco; mortuous plango; fulgura fango* (I call the living, I mourn the dead, I shiver the lightning), an inscription appropriate enough for an inn so near the church.

One of the regulars in the Spread Eagle assured me that royalty was not above staying in the inn in days gone by. He forgot who. And there was once a fine to-do here when a young and beautiful princess who had run away was found in this very inn!

Even when discovered she kept on running, but indoors her athletics were somewhat cramped and she was cornered in the long gallery upstairs—" couldn't rightly mind her name."

At one time Ingatestone had an inn called the Swan, which is still remembered in boxing circles because a celebrated fight took place in its yard in 1789. The contestants were Ingleston and Jackson. The latter was probably the better known, since he was trainer to the Prince of Wales, Byron and many a well-known gallant of the period.

The ring was set up in the yard the day before the match, but unfortunately rain fell during the night and the boards became slippery.

Odds were evens when the fight started, but Jackson's superior boxing skill soon revealed itself and the Ilford brewer was knocked down. But in the third round Jackson, now well in the lead, slipped on the boards, broke a small leg bone and dislocated an ankle. He was game enough to offer to continue the fight from a sitting position—provided, of course, that Ingleston would also assume the same unusual stance. His opponent, already declared the champion and, what was more important, being in possession of the purse, not unnaturally declined. Jackson's comments are unrecorded.

To the north of Ingatestone is Fryerning, and beyond the village is the Viper. It stands alone, overlooking the common which is still the haunt of the creature from which it derives its name. The sign is unique. The landlord will tell you that during the Hitler war he received letters from his soldier friends overseas addressed simply : " The Landlord, The Viper, England."

It is a cosy inn with no pretensions to arterial road-house splendour—which, of course, is as it should be. The interior decorations are of the simplest and no less effective for that reason. Indeed, the oft-forgotten point is here demonstrated that the wares themselves when arranged with imagination are the best decorations. The colours and shapes of the bottles, the variety of labels and the variegated beverages themselves can be used with striking effect.

On one of the many decorated jugs found on the shelves is the inscription (after John Ray, I believe) :

> " He that buys land—buys stones.
> He that buys flesh—buys bones.
> He that buys eggs—buys many ducks.
> He that buys ale—buys nothing else."

It is pleasant and peaceful at the Viper, and this fact is appreciated even more so when the Essex Great Road is regained at Margaretting—sweet name. South-east of the village is Margaretting Tye, where the White Hart has stood for some 200 years. For some years now harvest thanksgiving services have been held in the inn. People have flocked to the unusual service, and the bar, specially decorated with the riches of the soil for the occasion, looks particularly attractive.

We return to the main road and continue our journey towards Chelmsford. But at the River Wid we pause—not to admire the river, which is today a mere trickle, but to cast our minds back 500 years to Thomas Kemp.

Kemp was an actor of Shakespeare's time. Indeed, he knew the playwright well, and Shakespeare knew him too, for did he not insert into *Hamlet* the lines

> " Let those that play your clowns
> speak no more than is put down for them "

—to curb the extempore invention of Kemp? Not that such hints would have much effect on an actor who was as " brimful of mad jigges and merrie jests " as he was.

The maddest jig of his mad life started on the first Monday in Lent, 1599, for it was on that day that he set out from London with the intention of dancing to Norwich. He was accompanied by Tom Slye, whose job was to play a lively rhythm on his fife and tabor.

By Wednesday Kemp had reached Romford. Learning that it was market day in Brentwood the next day, he left early in the morning in order to arrive when the crowds were thickest. He did, for he said: " I had much adoe to get passage to my inne." After a brief rest he took advantage of the fine moonlight night to continue his capers to Ingatestone, accompanied, as always, by a crowd of spectators. On the following day this crowd became thinner as he approached Chelmsford. At Widford bridge—where, you will remember, we paused for reflection—" a number of country people, and many gentlemen and gentlewomen were gathered together to see me. Sir Thomas Mildmay, standing at his Parke pall, received gently, a payre of garters from me."

Here we must leave Kemp to continue his jig to Norwich, but we shall meet him again on our journey.

Nowadays, you seek in vain the Silent Woman of Widford. I refer to an inn, of course. On the sign it displayed the traditional headless woman, but for Miller Christy, whose book on Essex trade signs is invaluable, this was no joke. He regarded it as a piece of unwarrantable slander on the fair sex, being intended to convey the idea that a woman can be silenced only by being deprived of her head.

ROYAL OAK   HAVERING

CHAPTER IV

MANIE FAYRE INNES

IT was the bridge built by Bishop Maurice of London that stimulated the development of Chelmsford. Not that that was the bishop's intention! His sole purpose was to shorten the journey to his Chelmsford residence. His stone bridge made it unnecessary for him to follow the usual route through Writtle.

The advantages of the bridge soon became apparent, and from that day to this there has been a succession of bridges at this spot. It was natural, too, that inns should spring up at a later date at this important entrance to the town. One of the oldest, and certainly the most famous, of these was the Black Boy. From the fourteenth century until the year 1857 it stood in nearby Springfield Street where now stands its namesake. Not that it was an inn all that time. The discovery in the building of a boss of a blue boar combined with red and white roses does suggest that originally it was a residence of the de Veres. Not until the mid-sixteenth century was it recorded as an inn under the name of the Crown. This sign was adopted to commemorate the passing of the bishop's lands to the king. Before 1612, however, it had adopted the sign of the Black Boy, for an entry in the parish register for this year records the burial of " Elizabeth Scaston, Innholder at Black Boye, ye third day August 1612."

A room in the inn bore the royal arms above its door to indicate that it was the sheriff's prison. One of its unhappy occupants was Dr. Taylor, who was on his way from London to Hadleigh and the martyr's stake.

There is a tradition that Richard III caused his hunting party much concern. Thinking he was lost in the forest, they searched high and low, to discover him eventually passing the time pleasantly, and quite unconcerned about the trouble he was causing, in the Black Boy.

In 1669, Cosmo de Medici, later Grand Duke of Tuscany, also spent a pleasant night at the inn. We can assume that it was pleasant, for any place away from the cause of his travels—his wife!—was for him an agreeable haven. Later he was the guest of Lord Petre at Ingatestone Hall. He enjoyed the visit, but was not impressed by the English way of life. No French cook; no forks; no finger bowls! The pastry was " grossly made and badly done," and to round off the delightful meal the kitchen caught fire!

Among the numerous retinue accompanying the duke were one who found time to make a sketch of Chelmsford—the oldest still extant—and a Florentine named Sr. Bernard Gascoigne. When in Colchester the latter pointed out to his master the spot where, in 1648, he was almost shot when he and several others serving in the royalist forces were forced to surrender.

Sixty-seven years later other men of royalist sympathies stayed in the Black Boy. They were fifteen English gentlemen who, suspected of being Jacobites, were confined to the inn from October to December in the year 1715. Their " imprisonment " was to be envied at least from the gastronomical point of view. Generous friends regaled them with nineteen geese, 150 fowl, many hares, and large quantities of pork, beef and mutton! For beverages they had a choice of chocolate, coffee or tea and adequate supplies of ale. We are not told if they desired a quick release.

It was not until 1745 that the Long Room was thrown open to the public. Henceforth it was used for meetings and socials of all descriptions.

Fifty years later William of Orange, fleeing from Holland to London with his family, stayed overnight at the Black Boy. His presence was honoured by the bellringers of the town, but William left no monetary recognition. This meanness surprised the ringers— but enthusiasts do not always realize that everybody does not share their ardour for their tuneless changes.

No bells chimed for the Duke of Wellington when he changed horses at the Black Boy in October 1832. He was on his way to Sudbourne Hall to pay a visit to its owner, the Earl of Hereford.

It was not long after the duke's brief visit that a young girl paid an even briefer one—but one which had far-reaching consequences. The ostler on duty at the time was surprised to note that the rider of the panting, steaming horse was a girl. Hurriedly she changed horses and was off again along the road to London.

Margaret Catchpole was a most faithful servant in the household of the Rev. Richard Cobbold (who has told the story at some length). She was a good girl, but she loved Will Laud, a man who was known to the revenue officers because of his association with Tom Luff, a notorious smuggler. Will found these attentions rather disturbing, so he left the district to join the Navy. He proved an able sailor and actually obtained a free discharge. When, however, he returned to his former environment he soon drifted back into a life of crime.

It was at this time that Margaret received a letter from London purporting to come from Will, whom she still loved deeply. Mounting one of her master's horses, she headed for the City and covered the seventy-one miles in eight and a half hours! News of the escapade soon reached London and she was arrested, her identity being established by the ostler of the Black Boy. She was taken back to Ipswich, tried for horse stealing, and sentenced to death, but this was later commuted to seven years' banishment to Australia. No doubt she would have been released before deportation, but once again her lover came into her life. This time the rendezvous was the jail—for Will had been sentenced to a year's imprisonment and a £100 fine for committing a number of smuggling offences. At the end of the year Margaret paid the fine and Will was released.

At once he set about planning Margaret's escape. This did not prove too difficult, and the lovers hastened to the shore, where a boat was to meet them and take them to Holland. But the revenue officers had tracked them down, and Laud, attempting to resist arrest, was shot dead.

Tried for the second time, Margaret was found guilty, and in 1801 was deported to Australia for life.

Eleven years later Margaret married. By a strange twist of fate the man she married was the brother of the officer who had killed Will Laud! As in all good stories, they lived happily ever after, and by the time Margaret died in 1841 she had become a worthy citizen of Sydney.

In June 1835 Dickens stayed in the Black Boy. He was not impressed by Chelmsford, and that is quite understandable, for it rained all day and his only reading matter was a book on army field training. The experience was not forgotten. It was at this house that the novelist set the scene for the encounter of Tony

Weller and that "chevalier d'industrie" Alfred Jingle, and the ever-faithful Job. It was at the Black Boy that they mounted the coach that bore them to Ipswich and further adventures.

Twenty-five years after the visit of Dickens the inn was pulled down, William Atwells being the last, sad, landlord.

Near the Black Boy stood another ancient and well-known inn—the Cock. It was over 400 years old when it, too, was demolished. We remember it today because Foxe has immortalized its one-time landlord Richard Potto.

During the Marian purge, an itinerant preacher named Eagles, nicknamed Trudgeover because of his " immoderate and unseasonable going abroad," was apprehended near Colchester on a charge of treason, on which indictment he was found guilty and sentenced to be hanged, drawn and quartered.

" After the sentence had been pronounced he was carried to the Crown at Chelmsford, where Richard Potto the elder, of the Cocke, teased him to confess that he had in his prayer offended the Queen, and to ask forgiveness when he said he had not offended Her Grace. He was shortly afterwards placed upon a hurdle or sledge and drawn to the place of execution, being first bound, reading devoutly with a loud voice from a psalm book in his hand. Then the said Potto continued to tease him until the Sheriff commanded him to desist."

The unfortunate Trudgeover was still alive when he was cut down, so a bailiff of Chelmsford named Swallow dragged the body to a hurdle " and laid his neck thereon, and, with a cleaver, such as is occupied in many men's kitchens, and blunt, did hackle off his head and sometimes hit his neck, and sometimes his chin, and did foully mangle him."

Under the date 1558 there is an entry in the parish register which reads: " Pay'd at Putto's at the Coke, for ye clarke's brekefast when he came to help sing messe before ye justis of assice, XIII d."

A year after this entry was made Potto died. Let Foxe describe his end: " Though he lived until Queen Elizabeth's reign, he had little comfort, and then wrangling with two of his neighbours in his own house, and feeling himself not well, he desired a servant to accompany him to a chamber, when he fell on a low bed like a lump of lead, and foaming at the mouth, never spoke afterwards, being senseless for three or four days, and then died."

One cannot help thinking what a very good horror comic editor Foxe would have made!

A later landlord of the Cocke was a man called Browne, who was sufficiently interested in the town to lend money to support the performance of the miracle play which lasted several days during the feast of Corpus Christi. We know this from a warden's account of 1562: " Paid unto Goodman Browne, of Ye Cocke, for olde dette he lente at the first playe XLS."

Nicholas Sutton was another landlord of the same inn who became a churchwarden of St. Mary's. He and the landlord of the White Hart supplied the sacramental wine. The normal amount paid for bread and wine in one year was about thirty-eight shillings, but in 1625 we find that the sum of £8 was spent—a large amount when we remember that bread was one penny a loaf and wine eightpence a quart; but not so large when we realize that the Plague was serious in Chelmsford in 1625 and attendance at church increased as a consequence.

While on the subject of churches we must not forget that Chelmsford eccentric the Rev. G. S. Clarke. It was a practice of his to read his own translations of the Scriptures to his congregation. Naturally, he was inhibited by his bishop. Nothing daunted, he continued his readings in the same church, not from the pulpit, however, but from the opposite end of the church—much to the annoyance of his successor. The only method of silencing him was to place him in the local jail, and this is where he enters our story. From his cell window he could observe the comings and goings of all the coaches using the Ship inn, and so interested did he become in this activity that he recorded a wealth of interesting detail such as the times of arrival and departure and the colours of the horses and coaches.

In the year 1654 there were strange happenings in the White Horse. A full account is contained in a quarto tract now in the British Museum. The title page is self-explanatory:

" A true relation of a Horrid Murder, committed upon the Person of Thomas Kidderminster of Tupsley in the County of Hereford, Gent, at the White Horse Inn in Chelmsford, in the County of Essex, in the Month of April, 1654, together with a True Account of the Strange and Providential Discovery of the Same nine years after . . ."

Here I stop quoting or there will be little to tell!

Mrs. Kidderminster had heard no word of her husband for nine years. She knew that he had gone to Cambridge and that he intended returning to London via Chelmsford. In 1663 a friend showed her an announcement which said that some human bones had recently been discovered in a Chelmsford back yard. They could be those of her husband. With this vague belief troubling her mind she set out on foot for Chelmsford. That first night she reached Romford and put up at the Black Bull. There she met another woman also on her way to Chelmsford, and, not unnaturally, the conversation got round to the White Horse inn. The stranger knew the inn well. The present landlord was highly respected, but as for Sewell his predecessor, well, the less said about him the better. She would not be surprised if he turned out to be a murderer! No doubt his old ostler could say a lot if he had a mind to.

But the old ostler had no mind to. He refused the women's request to call on them, so on to Chelmsford they trudged. The first place they called at was the White Horse. Mrs. Sewell was no longer the landlady—she had moved to the Shears. Like her one-time ostler she had nothing to say.

Back to Romford to Moses Drayne, the ostler. This time he did talk a little. Yes, he did recall a man of the description of Mr. Kidderminster. Yes, there was a chambermaid at the White Horse. She was Mary Kendall and she now lived in Brentwood.

Mrs. Kidderminster now felt she had enough information to call in the police. Moses Drayne and Mary were arrested. Mary's evidence was damning. On the night of the crime she had been moved to a bedroom in a remote part of the inn and her door had been locked until the following morning. Next day she was told that the traveller had left and this she believed, but when she found that the door of his room was kept locked for several weeks she became suspicious. Eventually she did have an opportunity to glance in and she recognized some garments belonging to the missing man. When she showed these to Mrs. Sewell she was beaten, and in the ensuing row it became obvious that Mr. Kidderminster had been murdered in order to obtain the £600 he was carrying.

Mrs. Sewell and Moses Drayne were proved to be accomplices in the murder and Drayne was hanged.

There are no tales of murder associated with two of the old

inns that still remain in Chelmsford—the White Hart and the Saracen's Head, both standing near the Shire Hall. The only unsavoury incident that is recorded took place in the White Hart when a thief was arrested there by the Bow Street runners. He had stolen the church plate and had hidden it under the bed for the night. The inn was a well-known coaching house and relics of those days still remain, though somewhat changed. Where once rolled coaches now run cars, and the former stables have been converted into an attractive bar.

The Saracen's Head has a dignified Georgian exterior. This inn is mentioned several times in Strutt's *Queenhoo Hall*. In one passage the hero says: " On my arrival at Chelmsford, I went to one of the principal inns, distinguished by the sign of the Saracen, or Man Quintain, where I took some small refreshment." But it is with that greater novelist Anthony Trollope that the Saracen's Head will be for ever associated. As an official in the surveyor's department of the Post Office he travelled extensively throughout Essex. Frequently he devoted his evenings to correcting proofs of his books. On one occasion when staying at the Saracen's Head he overheard two clergymen discussing his current novel which was appearing in serial form. The main complaint was that the same characters kept cropping up in all the novels, which could be irksome if the characters were unpopular.

" Confound that Mrs. Proudie! I wish she were dead! " exclaimed one of the clergymen with some heat.

Hearing this, Trollope could contain himself no longer. " Gentlemen, she shall die in the next number."

Later he was sorry that he had made the promise. In his autobiography he wrote: " It was with many misgivings that I killed my old friend. I have sometimes regretted the deed."

CHAPTER V

CHARMS OF AN INN

THE Trollope incident has been questioned by many authorities—a genus ever ready to spoil the best stories! They have also denied that Goldsmith ever stayed at Springfield, although the local tradition that a large part of *The Deserted Village* was composed in the neighbourhood is a long time a-dying. So the Endeavour might have been known to him. Even if he did not know the area the ghosts of other great ones haunt the roads around these parts. Henry VIII frequently travelled to New Hall, Boreham, to entertain one of his post-Boleyn lady loves. He had seized the estate from her father after her death and on it started to build the magnificent hall he called New, although most of the building we now see was the work of Thomas Radcliffe, Earl of Sussex. George Villiers, Duke of Buckingham, Oliver Cromwell and General Monk all lived there. So did Henry VIII's daughters. It was here that Mary entertained Lady Jane Grey a few years before signing her death warrant.

We pass through Boreham, with its White Hart, and Hatfield Peverel, with its Swan, and arrive in Witham. Did so attractive a town ever have such an unattractive approach? Beyond the gasworks, however, we are in another world, the eighteenth-century world of coaches, ladies and their gallants, for many of the houses that line the High Street were built in that age, and many long before.

After the rigid mould of council estates, how delightful to see such variety of design and material. Here we have façades of weatherboard, plaster, tiles, brick and roughcast. Here we have a dozen colours, a dozen roof styles and a multitude of chimney shapes. So great is the charm that we are not surprised to see such a " period piece " as the Spread Eagle crowning the High Street. Even the appearance of a stage-coach turning sharply into the inn yard would not seem strange. Thirteenth-century gables still overlook the High Street, but inside the inn has been much restored.

The tradition is strong that the Spread Eagle had close ties with the east-coast smugglers. Its proximity to that famed haunt of the underworld Tiptree Heath lends credence to the belief. It is said that contraband left in the inn was concealed in a secret well which could be reached only through a passage in the roof.

Near the Spread Eagle stands the White Hart. It has a striking sign. Seen against the soft evening sky it is at its most attractive, for then the hart, " crowned and gorged or," stands out impressively. The White Hart is an ancient house dating back some 500 years. In the days of the Tudors it lodged the Home Guard of those days—the Trained Bands, which were ever ready to rush at a moment's notice to defend the coast. Inside the huge chimney in the dining room is a recess used in days gone by to dry the wood for making bows and arrows. On one of the original oak beams is carved a Tudor rose inside a horseshoe, indicating that someone, maybe a former landlord, took part in that colourful spectacle the Field of the Cloth of Gold.

Among the many items to be seen in one of the bars is a poster advertising the " First Meeting of the Witham Labourers' Friendly Agricultural Society, Thursday, 9th October, 1845." The list of competitions makes interesting reading. In it are the three that follow, but not the headings.

Drunk in charge!

" To the Waggoner who has had the care of a team of Horses, not less than three, for the longest uninterrupted period with the same employer, or in the same occupation, regard being had to sobriety and conduct on the road."

Ambiguity!

" To the Domestic Man Servant who shall have lived the greatest number of years with one Master or Mistress."

Consolation prize!

" To the labourer in Husbandry who shall have brought up the largest family without Parochial Relief £2. 0. 0d."

In the inn yard, now used as a car park, is a thatched aviary.

The inn called the Blue Posts was probably the one most noted as a posting house until the advent of the railway to Witham, but it seems that after that event the business passed to the White Hart and the Albert.

The latter inn stands in that part of Witham known as Chipping

Hill. Chipping is the ancient word for market, and there is no need to look far to discover the reason for that market, for nearby stands the Woolpack. Its sign is as nothing compared with the striking effigy which stands outside the Albert—a giant blackamoor clad in a Lamour-like sarong. He wears a golden crown, a necklace and a moustache to match. His outstretched arm once held a spear. The landlord thinks that the giant was once a ship's figurehead and that it was placed in its present position about sixty years ago. This may be true, but one cannot help thinking that here is a sign that would have done credit to the famous Black Boy in Chelmsford.

Chipping Hill has an ancient name but modern ways, for its White Horse boasts a television bar.

The inn mentioned above—the Blue Posts—features in the *Journal of a Very Young Lady*. She described in rhyme a journey she made in the September of 1804 from Cannonbury to Aldborough and back via Harwich, Colchester, etc.

> " Travellers frequently boast of the charms of an inn,
>   But the Blue Post at Witham's the best I have seen;
>   The rooms are so clean, so delicious the diet,
>   The landlord so civil, so spruce and so quiet,
>   The servants all round so desirous to please
>   That you find yourself here most completely at ease.
>   We supped and we slept and we breakfasted too,
>   And then bid to Witham a parting adieu."

Doggerel maybe, but what a delightful description of the ideal inn.

Half-way between Witham and Kelvedon stands Rivenhall, famous as the birthplace of Thomas Tusser, contemporary of " Madde Jigges " Kemp and author of *Five Hundred Points of Good Husbandrie*. He was a living example of Shaw's dictum. He was a complete failure as a practical farmer, so he taught others how to farm!

The Angel occupies a corner in Kelvedon—" the very devil of a corner," as Israel Alexander, the noted Jewish whip, called it. William III frequently stayed at the Angel on his journeys to and from Holland. Farther along the High Street, Charles Haddon Spurgeon was born in a house that originally formed part of an inn called the Wheatsheaf. What a personality and what a preacher was Spurgeon! His father and grandfather were preachers too, but their oratory paled beside his. He started preaching at the age of sixteen and four years later he was offered a London pulpit. His fame spread rapidly and soon no hall was big enough to hold his congregations. Eventually a temple was built specially for him at a cost of £31,000, this sum being subscribed in one month. Congregations of 7,000 were common, and when he preached in the Crystal Palace at the time of the Indian Mutiny 24,000 came to hear him— and this without the aid of modern publicity methods. His sermons reached a vast unseen congregation too, since they were printed weekly and the pamphlet was sold at a penny. Add to all this the flood of books from his pen—books which sold at a phenomenal rate—and some measure of his terrific influence can be gauged.

A bridge crosses the Blackwater and leads into Feering. Looking back we see the Railway Tavern—symbol of an age!—standing prominently on the river bank. Nearby is the Sun inn, with its carved bressumers and barge-boards. Inside are a magnificent chimney beam and a pilastered parlour. The Sun has stood here for centuries and among the scores of notabilities who must have seen it are Queen Elizabeth I, Bishop Bonner and Bishop Ridley, for they all stayed some time in the neighbouring hamlet of Feering Bury. Constable, too, was no stranger to the place. He was friendly with the rector, Mr. Driffield, who, said the painter, " christened me, one night in great haste, about eleven o'clock."

Up the hill from the Sun is the Old Anchor road house, a splendid example of medieval architecture but with beams painted on the plaster façade!

The road continues straight on to Marks Tey, standing at the junction of the Harwich road and Stane Street. Such a position should have encouraged the growth of a town, according to my geography text-books, but all we find are a few houses and the solitary Trowel and Hammer.

GOAT & BOOT · COLCHESTER

CHAPTER VI

COLCHESTER

BEYOND Marks Tey we soon realize that we are approaching Colchester—and anyone with a sense of history must feel a tingle of anticipation, for the present-day traveller is, like his predecessors of long, long ago, seeking warmth and shelter among his fellows within the town walls of Camulodunum.

Once inside these walls, we who are in quest of hostelries are faced with many difficulties, not the least being the historical richness of the town. Seek an inn, you find a church; track down a Roman remain, you find a Norman relic. But one has to be single-minded to make any progress, so let us follow in the tracks of the London coach as it whirled into the town and whoa!—here we are at the Red Lion.

And well our single-mindedness has been repaid, for here is a gem of inn architecture standing between two other inns of almost equal fame—the George and the Three Cups.

The Red Lion did not start its long life as an inn, however. Originally it was a private residence of the Howards. Nor did it start its social life as a *red* lion. Formerly it was known as the Whyght Lion, the colour of the Howards. The change occurred when the Scottish James ascended the English throne. Just before this event a manuscript of 1603-4 records that " the Lyon, the Aungel and the Whyte Hart were appointed the only three wyne taverns in ye towne being aincyent Innes and Tavernes."

With a feeling of disappointment we must record that the Red Lion is not as " aincyent " as the Roman mosaic pavement found on the site. The oldest features of the present building are probably the fourteenth-century stone doorway and some masonry in the vaulted cellars. It has been claimed, with very little proof, that these remnants are part of a monastic establishment. Largely, the main structure is of the fifteenth century, although additions and alterations have taken place throughout the intervening years.

Most of the wonderful timber work was concealed for a great length of time beneath layers of wallpaper and plaster. As purists we must decry such bad taste, but at the same time we must not forget that this vandalism frequently preserved much fine craftsmanship for the enjoyment of later generations.

The front of the Red Lion is a delight, with its half-timbered overhanging gables and traceried panels. Inside, too, there is ancient moulded timber in grill room and dining room. In the latter is a king-post. The first-floor landing has the tracery of a fifteenth-century window and the upstairs lounge finely moulded beams.

The Red Lion was among the first inns used by the London coaches. We have evidence that one was running as early as 1756. Not only stage-coaches made the journey; post-chaises and stage-carts catered for people of varied means.

From an ancient order of the city fathers we learn that " the pease and roote market with the onions, garlick and cucumbers shall be holden and kept from the Lyon downward towards St. Nicholas Church and in no other place." It is likely, then, that the Red Lion was the inn meant by Foxe when he wrote that Edward Freese was caught adding scriptural texts to some cloths he was painting for the inn situated " in the middle of the market place." For such action Freese was accused of being a heretic. He was captured in the inn-yard, taken to London and imprisoned " with certain others of Essex, that is, to wit, one Johnson and his wife; Wylie and his wife and son; and father Bate of Rowhedge.

" After the painter had been there a long spare, by much suit he was removed to Lollard's Tower. His wife, in the time of the suit, where he met at Fulham, being desirous to see her husband, and pressing to come in at the gate, being great with child, the porter lifted up his foot and struck her on the body, that at length she died of the same; but the child was destroyed immediately . . .

" This painter would ever be writing on the walls with chalk or coal, and in one place he wrote, ' Doctor Dodipall would make me believe the moon were made of green cheese.' To prevent this writing he was manacled, which caused his arms to swell. The conditions of his imprisonment eventually drove him to insanity, at which point he was released and sent back to his home in Yorkshire. Alas! poor man, he never regained his sanity and home was no longer home to him and he would not tarry there."

Step across the High Street from the Tudor Red Lion and you enter the Georgian Cups. Do not be misled by the modern exterior. Behind it is much nineteenth-century work—and even earlier. The most notable room in the Three Cups, or Cups as it is often called, is the one which was designed to be the principal hall and ballroom in Colchester. This elegant Renaissance room, complete with musicians' gallery, was opened in 1807 when Louis XVIII of France stayed at the inn. He was not the only royal visitor; George IV also stayed there. This is not surprising, since the Cups was the principal mail and coaching house of Colchester.

Quite near the Cups on the same side of the High Street is the George, an inn incorporating a number of ancient features. The courtyard is entered through an eighteenth-century gatehouse, which is a fine example of the timberwork of the period, and at the head of the Georgian staircase is a king-post which appears to be a vestige of a fifteenth-century hall.

But to see medieval woodcraft at its finest a visit to the Marquis of Granby on North Hill is called for. The actual marquis was not medieval. He lived in the eighteenth century, becoming commander-in-chief of the British Army in 1766, and many an inn changed its name to honour the popular soldier. Incidentally, he gave rise to a well-known phrase. In his day it was customary to wear wigs, even in battle, but this practice found no favour with the bald marquis—hence the phrase " to go into something baldheaded."

The skill of the woodcarver is to be admired in the Tudor billiard room. The great oak beam spanning the room is carved with eagles, dragons, dogs and monkeys. At either end its wall-posts are decorated with carvings of lively figures of men in sixteenth-century costume. In the centre of the beam are some initials which can be read as H.M. or H.W. Much ink has been used in an attempt to determine the owner of these letters. One feasible suggestion is that they stand for Henry Webbe, who was a prominent Colchester clothier and merchant flourishing round about 1500.

Over the fireplace is a carved panel showing, it is said, the seven sinners. Each is enclosed in a disc and these are linked together with running foliage. On the wall above the fireplace is a bas-relief designed by that well-known citizen of Colchester Gurney Benham, portraying historical persons connected with the town's history sitting down to the celebrated oyster feast.

Climbing North Hill, we arrive at the Fleece, another coaching inn which has been attractively modernized. The coach entrance is centrally situated and above it is the sign carved in stone.

The nearby King's Head occupies a unique position surmounting that remarkable Roman relic the Balkerne Gate. The contrast between these two structures strikes one as being extremely odd—just as if Cæsar were portrayed wearing a bowler!

The great gateway was erected about A.D. 80, that is about twenty years after my compatriot Boudicca had destroyed the town. It is about 100 feet wide and projects about thirty feet in front of the Roman wall. Originally there were two guardrooms and four passageways, two for pedestrians and two for vehicles.

The King's Head itself is not very old, but its predecessor was quite ancient. Foxe informs us that during the persecutions " at the Kinge's Head in Colchester, and at other innes in the said towne, the afflicted Christians had set places appointed for them to meet at."

The former King's Head stood in Head Street, and it was from this inn, according to Matthew Carter, quartermaster-general of the royalist forces, that Sir Charles Lucas and Sir George Lisle walked together for the last time to the castle and their death. The siege by Fairfax had been long—seventy-six days—and the defenders had shown great courage. The execution of the royalist leaders still arouses heated arguments. Indeed, it was in the bar of the King's Head that I overheard a latter-day Roundhead and an equally fervent Royalist abuse each other in violent terms over this very incident that took place not last week but some 300 years ago!

What of the inns that are no more? Some, like the Angel in West Stockwell Street, have merely changed their occupations; others, like the Swan and the White Hart, are now but names in the town's history.

The Angel was appropriately named. It was built as an inn to house the overflow of the abbey of St. John the Baptist. We know it existed as early as 1517, and in 1603 it was one of the three wine taverns of Colchester. In those days, too, it was the scene of official banquets of the town bailiffs and aldermen. This gem of medieval architecture was one of the smaller posting and coaching houses of the town.

The Swan inn stood in Frere Street near the east gate, a position

SE AND CROWN   COLCHESTER

THE KINGS HE
COLCHESTE

which made it a favourite stopping place of travellers from Harwich. It ceased being an inn round about the time that Shakespeare died.

At the top of the High Street on the south side stood the White Hart. It was a large building containing a main hall which according to the son of the Duc de Liancourt, who stayed there with Arthur Young in July 1784, was seventy-four feet long by thirty-four feet wide. Inevitably a hall of these dimensions was used as a meeting place by the numerous Colchester societies—Turnpike Trustees, Association of Horse Dealers, etc.—and as a venue for balls and dinners. This varied patronage helped to augment the never-ceasing bustle of this coaching and posting inn.

Of the many landlords of the White Hart none is more memorable than Christopher White. He was not born or bred to the job. Farming was his occupation until he moved into the inn in 1782. His stay in the White Hart was short, however—just four years! But he did not abandon the hotel business; he moved to Paris and opened there the Philadelphia, although it soon became known as White's. On November 18, 1792, a celebrated meeting took place in the hotel. Tom Paine presided. He had but recently fled from England, where his *Rights of Man* had just been published. Others present were a former Member of Parliament for Colchester, Sir Robert Smyth, Bart., Lord Edward Fitzgerald, a son of the Duke of Leinster, and a banker of Paris. It was the banker who proposed the toast " to the abolition of hereditary titles "— and Lord Edward acted at once.

Some years before Christopher White became landlord of the White Hart, Boswell and Johnson probably stayed one night in the inn. The year was 1763. The *Life* simply states that on Friday, August 5, they set out early in the morning in the Harwich stage-coach and " stopped a night in Colchester." Considering the importance of the White Hart at that time, it is safe to assume that that is where they stayed. It was during this brief sojourn in Colchester that Johnson uttered the well-known words: " Some people have a foolish way of not minding, or pretending to mind, what they eat. For my part, I mind my belly very studiously, and very carefully; for I look upon it that he who does not mind his belly will hardly mind anything else."

THE LAMB · DEDHAM

CHAPTER VII

THROUGH DEDHAM VALE

ONE is reluctant to leave Colchester, so varied are its riches, but the anticipation of what lies beyond the town— the country made immortal by the brush of Constable—is sufficiently strong to overcome the counter-attractions of Camu lodunum.

Beyond the castle is a small inn known as the Goat and Boot. A former landlord possessed a unique, if gruesome, relic—the skeleton of a four-year-old boy displayed in a glass case. It seems that the unfortunate boy had been trapped between the inner and outer walls of a barge and had died a slow and painful death.

A short distance beyond the Goat and Boot, where the Roman road branches off to Ipswich, stands a magnificent Elizabethan house occupying the bend of the road. It is the Rose and Crown. It delights with its variety. Its irregular roof of rich red tiles, its varied gables, its black and white façade and its numerous openings all harmonize into something rich and strange.

After the noise and bustle of Colchester the rural peace along almost the entire road to Harwich comes as a surprise. The villages are small and far apart, and accordingly the inns are few in number. Ardleigh possesses two, the quaintly named Wooden Fender and the Red Lion. The latter occupies a corner site in the village overlooking the magnificent medieval church porch. Renovators have done their best to obliterate signs of age in the Red Lion, but ancient beams, like the grey hairs on a much-dyed lady, peep through.

The old coach road runs through Lawford to Manningtree but dull would be he who could pass by Dedham and the Stour for this is Constable country, the scene of some of his greatest paintings. Indeed, it was his " Dedham Vale " that first brought him to the fore as a major artist. We walk these roads and view these scenes and ancient buildings with added pleasure since we know that Constable must have enjoyed them too. He would have known the great church with its unusual tower; he would have known the Sun inn standing opposite. The tall coach entrance invites one inside to a world of yesterday. When is it at its most charming? That is, perhaps, a matter of taste. I was there on a summer evening when the sunlight flickered through the fan-finger leaves of the great chestnut and the doves were cooing lazily on the red roofs of the old buildings. The dovecot is attached to an external staircase, a feature unique in Essex. I believe that the only other of its kind in England is to be found in faraway Gloucester, in the New Inn of that city.

The Marlborough Head is the other Dedham inn, and a fine example of half-timber work it is, too. The freedom—I almost said the abandon—with which the inn timbers were erected is something to be wondered at.

On the outskirts of the village, on the border of Suffolk, is the Gun inn. It has the distinction of being one of the few inns to be marked on Chapman and André's map of 1777. It is the last inn in Essex—or the first!—and in the olden days was patronized chiefly by the poorer traveller who could not afford to stay in the Colchester inns.

Its position made it a favourite rendezvous for sportsmen of both counties. Cock-fights were held here, and the long-room was the scene of many a pleasant social gathering. One memorable occasion was after the newly installed bells were rung in Dedham church on November 1, 1754.

One leaves Dedham with pleasant memories, and one of the most pleasant is the fact that the villagers have resisted the temptation to commercialize the great painter. No " Constable Cake Shoppe," no plaques to record where the great man stood or slept or painted. Can there be any other town in England that has resisted such a temptation?

We have been lured already from the main Harwich road in order to visit the Constable country, and once again we stray— this time into another county. Who can resist crossing a border, particularly when the transgression leads us to a place like Flatford Mill? But we must resist the attraction of these delights or our journey will be endless, so we recross the Stour and enter Man-ningtree.

The main street of Manningtree seems to be squeezed between the buildings on either side—buildings which vary between simple cottages built in typical style and the surprisingly large and imposing post office. In the coaching era there were two important inns in the town, the White Hart and the Packet. The latter is no longer an inn, but a Ministry of Labour office, although the yard attached to the building is still known as the Packet yard. The petty sessions were held in the inn in its heyday.

The White Hart is still thriving and there is no mistaking its former business. The coach entrance opens into the former yard, still lined with the buildings of yesteryear. The inn sign is a feeble effort illustrating what one might describe as a *hart filleted*. At one time there must have been a more imposing sign, for a local poet who combined teetotalism with the writing of doggerel—although I am assured the relation is purely coincidental!—wrote the following:

> " Its sign is carved on wood, a Hart reclined,
> And by a golden chain it seems confined;
> For fear perchance it might on some fine day
> Escape, and bound o'er hill and dale away."

Why is it that the two books *Maria Monk in a Monastery* and *Maria Marten and the Murder in the Red Barn* should be almost as well known as the works of Shakespeare? They enjoy a fame out of all proportion to their literary value. The question is prompted by the fact that there is a slight connection between Maria Marten and the White Hart. Corder, her lover and murderer, stayed one night at the inn after he had committed the crime. He also cashed a forged cheque at the local bank. So when some time later he was arrested, the landlord, Nathaniel Dale, and the chief clerk, Mr Taylor, were called in to identify the murderer, who was being held under arrest in the Colchester George.

When I visited the inn, some regulars were discussing totalitarian methods of extracting confessions, and I could not help recalling that one of the arch-exponents of the practice was a local man called Matthew Hopkins, the seventeenth-century witch hunter. For every witch he discovered he was paid twenty shillings. His method was quite simple, the " no-sleep " method, made all too familiar by the recent spate of anti-nazi and anti-communist books. The victim became so exhausted by being kept awake that she confessed to any crime suggested in order to obtain the sleep for which she yearned. Eventually the witch hunter's methods caused a revulsion of feeling among decent people, and he met with the same fate as he had meted out to others.

Beyond Manningtree stand the twin towers designed by Robert Adam, now serving as a memorial to his sole attempt at church designing.

Why Robert Adam should have built a church in this remote part of Essex may appear puzzling, but it must be remembered that in the eighteenth century Mistley was a popular rendezvous of the young bloods, attracted by the lavish hospitality of the witty and convivial Squire Rigby.

Rigby's grandfather first built a house in Mistley, and it was to this that his son retired after some successful speculating in the South Sea Company. His father's house proved too small for his tastes, so he had it rebuilt on a grander scale, at the same time changing the banks of the quiet river into a bustling commercial centre by the erection of warehouses, granaries and wharves.

His son, the Right Hon. Richard Rigby, inherited his father's wealth but not his business acumen. Gambling and heavy drinking further reduced the fortune and it was not long before he found himself in financial straits. At this crucial point he had a remarkable stroke of luck, for when the Duke of Bedford was attacked by thugs on Lichfield racecourse he was saved by the courageous intervention of the spendthrift heir. This prompt and brave action assured his advancement. From then on it was roses, roses all the way—Master of the Rolls for Ireland, Vice-Treasurer and finally Paymaster to the Forces. This last was a most lucrative appointment. During his sixteen years of office he amassed a fortune of half a million pounds.

Such wealth allied to such a character as Rigby's could produce but one result. Mistley Hall became " Liberty Hall," where all Rigby's acquaintances and hangers-on savoured the sort of life that many of them could not afford. Like a celebrated London theatre of our own day it " never closed." By day and by night guests arrived or departed and the life of the quiet villages was enlivened—and endangered—by the driving of young blades well primed with brandy.

The towers that prompted this digression were built about 1744. The great architect was commissioned to redesign the house and to beautify the town. Today the twin towers and the bedraggled swan fountain are among the few vestiges of Adam's work. Rigby's hall has long since disappeared.

Beyond the church and beyond the malting works lining the Stour is an inn with magic in its name—the Mistley Thorn. But the exterior is disappointing, quite different from the idea the name conveys. The interior, however, is more interesting. The coach entrance still exists and leads to the stables where Squire Rigby's surplus guests left their horses. It was only recently that the pump was removed from the present living room to make way for mod. cons. The present scullery was used at one time as a mortuary, and it is not unlikely that stories of this room being haunted date from this fact. Religious services, too, have been held in the inn.

Today the Mistley Thorn is a museum in miniature. Every room contains objects of interest and beauty: Chinese vases, exquisitely carved tables from India, wishing chairs from China—cargo for a quinquireme!

From the upper rooms the Stour can be glimpsed between the buildings of the huge maltings. Smugglers used the river, and tales of their prowess are still heard in Mistley and Manningtree. Many a knowing local will point to the cock-lofts in the older houses, will talk of mists on the river and of rides by night. As we continue on our journey to Harwich over the lonely, twisting, undulating roads it is not difficult to imagine customs officers hot in pursuit of their prey, or to picture white-clothed figures dashing through the night so that all good people would turn their faces to the wall— for fear of the " ghost "—and see naught of the contraband runners.

Houses are few and far between and inns are equally scarce. At Bradfield is the quaintly named Stranger's Home. The judge who tried the judges who tried Charles I lived in this village. He was Sir Harbottle Grimstone. That was his real name, and not one coined by Dickens!

Harwich is not far away now. Can you imagine the coach passengers waiting eagerly for their first glimpse of the town and of the sea beyond? Theirs had been a long journey. The roads left much to be desired, and in winter the loneliness and the wildness on parts of the route made them yearn for the comfort and the warmth of a Harwich inn. And inns there were in plenty.

Harwich in its heyday as an important port, dockyard and garrison town was well supplied with inns and public-houses. Even today thirty-five inns for a town of its size is not inconsider-

able, but is only about half the number of the " good old days."
As one would expect, many signs have a nautical flavour—the
Nelson, the British Flag, the Lifeboat and the Alma. Many old
and famous signs swing no more, but the White Hart and the Three
Cups are still there to link us with the past.

Of the many great men who patronized the Three Cups, perhaps
the greatest was Nelson. Until the " improvements " to the inn
were carried out, the Nelson room was a place of pilgrimage for
all admirers of the great admiral. Alas, the room is no more!
Incredible as it may seem, it was completely destroyed when the top
part of the inn was renewed. Even the Nelson relics were dispersed.

It is a comforting thought that no modern brewery company
would commit such sacrilege nowadays. They are all too aware of
the custom they would be destroying. The few vestiges of antiquity
still to be seen in the Three Cups—Elizabethan beams chiefly—
are hardly sufficient to compensate for the historic loss. One
wonders why the beams were overlooked!

We have already met Johnson and Boswell in Colchester. Where
they stayed when they arrived in Harwich is not known with
certainty, but the Three Cups is not an unlikely place. We know
that it stood near the church, and the doctor's piety was " constant
and fervent." Boswell records that they did attend church and that
on returning to their inn they discussed Bishop Berkeley's ingenious
sophistry to prove the non-existence of matter. " I observed," said
Boswell, " that though we are satisfied that his doctrine is not true,
it is impossible to refute it. I never shall forget the alacrity with
which Johnson answered, striking his foot with mighty force
against a large stone, till he rebounded from it, ' I refute it thus.' "

The other noted coaching house of Johnson's time was the
White Hart. It still possesses many features of its former days,
now much camouflaged. The stables had to be altered when the
railway was extended to the quay, but the archways can still be
seen above the chicken runs. The original coach entrance is partly
occupied by the main entrance. Enter by this doorway and you are
greeted by a most unusual sight. The one-time central courtyard
is now roofed with glass and a gallery runs round the first floor.
From two corners of this light and airy hall grow two vines, writhing
their way upwards to the glass roof. In season, huge bunches of
luscious grapes hang temptingly from the branches. And the secret
of such fertility? Beer slops and barrel dregs!

There is a tradition that Charles I planted the vines and that cuttings from them were later taken back to Hampton Court.

A well still exists in the inn. It is in the courtyard and is now covered by a trap-door. In a room overlooking the well Dr. Crippen is said to have once stayed.

About five years ago the White Hart ceased to be an inn. More recently the local Labour Party adapted the ground floor to serve as a social club, while the upper floor was converted into flats.

It is a fascinating experience to wander round the narrow streets of Harwich, slipping down narrow passages, glimpsing the sea beneath beetling stories, absorbing some of the spirit of the place, dreaming of the ghosts of the countless sailors, famous and infamous, who have also wandered along these ways—sailors of the *Mayflower*, sailors of Nelson's fleet, sailors of the two world wars. All of them would have known the White Hart, and no doubt many would have swallowed a " Nelson's blood " in the Globe, which stands hard by the quay. It is not on the sea front, but near enough to enjoy the salt tang and, less pleasantly, to be flooded when the seas run high. It is a picturesque inn with its beetling stories, its gables and its *Treasure Island* atmosphere. Inside are old beams, and upstairs the ceilings are decorated with plaster motifs of fleur-de-lys, Tudor roses and unusual carbuncle shapes.

Defoe, when he visited Harwich, complained of the extravagant reckonings of its public-houses. Today he would find Harwich no different in this respect from the other towns of Essex.

SUN INN
DEDHAM

The PELDON "ROSE"

CHAPTER VIII

BACK OF THE BEYOND

SOUTH of Harwich is a region that can best be described in the phrase of that well-known Essex writer S. L. Bensusan—" back of the beyond." The bustle and animation of Harwich and the Essex Great Road are soon forgotten in the peace of this changeless countryside. Despite the popularity of Walton-on-the-Naze and Clacton, this land lying between the Stour on the north and the Colne on the south has changed but little since the great days of the smugglers. Indeed, it requires but little imagination when wandering at night through the lonely lanes to picture those old smugglers creeping stealthily from the creekside rendezvous bent double beneath their ill-gotten gains. In the quiet inns of this quiet countryside a receptive ear hears many a tale told with relish by men who are everything you imagine a smuggler to be, for these marshes make tough men, men of resource, quiet in manner but determined and ever ready for action. These same men who sit quietly over their pints will weather the fierce North Sea gales, accepting the worst that nature can give with stoic resignation, or maybe that very night they will be shrouded in the dank, rheumy mists of the marshes awaiting the approach of duck or geese.

To those accustomed to the sardine-like existence of towns, the emptiness of these Essex lowlands is hard to imagine. Villages are few in number and always small. In summer time they are quiet enough, but in winter, particularly at night, the silence is heavy.

The road from Harwich to Walton winds its way inland to avoid the creeks and saltings of Hamford Water. Between the trees or over the high hedges it is always possible to glimpse the gleam of water—a reminder that those who live in the " back of the beyond " may have one foot on the land but the other is usually in the sea. Small paths leave the villages and wind down to the saltings. Stand on the water's edge and the only sounds you hear

are the seagull's cry and the lap-lapping of the water—while a
few miles away at Walton and Frinton thousands of holiday-
makers crowd the beaches.

Back on the winding road, and we arrive in Great Oakley. In
the *Chelmsford Chronicle* for 1787 there appeared the following
announcement: "Cocking. On Friday, March 9th, will be fought
a Main of Cocks, at the sign of the Castle, Great Oakley, for two
Guineas a Battle, and Five the odds; where the company of all
gentlemen and others will be esteemed a favour, by their humble
servant, William Rayner. The Cocks to be pitted at eleven o'clock,
and a good ordinary to be provided at two."

In Beaumont, Lord Byng lies buried. He would have known
Thorpe-le-Soken with its two inns—the 400-year-old Bell with its
two gables and carved bressumers, and the Rose and Crown with
its Dutch-type end gables.

Carved on the screen in the south aisle of the church is an
Elizabethan inscription: "This loft is the bachelers made by ales."

This is but one of the many references to church ales to be found
in Essex. These ales or aleings were the forerunners of the present-
day bazaars and garden fêtes, although they were, it is safe to
assume, much more hectic. Their purpose was primarily to raise
funds for the church, as the inscription quoted above indicates,
or as Peter Mews, royalist Bishop of Winchester, put it in his
" Ex-ale-tation of Ale ":

> " The churches much owe, as we all do knowe,
> For when they be drooping and ready to fail,
> By a Whitsun or Church-Ale up again they shall go,
> And owe their repairing to a pot of good ale."

This doggerel was written 100 years after a canon had forbidden
such activities in the church. Evidently it had had little effect, for
an aleing was such an easy way—and an enjoyable one, we must
add!—of raising money. The enthusiasm of both organizers and
participants seems to have known no bounds.

Whenever the church fabric, furniture or accessories required
repair an aleing was organized, and continued until the necessary
funds were obtained. To raise money for the church was a noble
task, but this end was defeated if those who took part destroyed
church property. This is clearly indicated in another canon of
1683: "The churchwardens or guestemen and their assistants

shall suffer no plays, feasts, banquets, suppers, church-ale drinkings . . . in the church, chapel or churchyard.''

We can be reasonably certain that even this enactment failed to eradicate entirely the consumption of ale on church premises. The church took a liberal view of drinking provided moderation was observed. In many a church register in Essex we read of the vestry adjourning to the local, the expenses being charged to the church. And Kipling's suggestion that vicar and smuggler were no strangers was not a figment of the poet's imagination.

At Thorpe-le-Soken we turn inland to Weeley, a village built on a green island surrounded by roads. It is almost plumb in the centre of this Essex promontory, so it is a pity that the appropriately named Hub inn is no more. Instead we have the more modern Black Boy. There is little to distinguish the inns of the surrounding villages. They attract neither by their architecture nor by their history. They are just village inns with no pretensions to fame. They were built to serve the villagers, and this they have done well for centuries and no doubt will do so for many centuries to come. They are like friendly dogs of indeterminate pedigree, not strikingly attractive but of surprising warmth and friendliness. If, then, we pass through villages and make no mention of the inns, that is not because they have no merit but simply because their presence is accepted as an essential part of the English scene. When that friendly dog dies how we miss it!

At the mouth of the Colne stands Brightlingsea, a delightfully peaceful seaside place, with a broad main street from which lesser streets run down to the river. Shipbuilding, oysters and holiday-makers are the chief industries of this former Cinque Port. There are pleasant inns in the town although a number such as the White Lion and the Duke have closed down. The Two Brewers is weather-boarded and tiled; the innocent Rosebud could probably tell many a tale of smuggling days; the Freemason's Arms has an unusual rear entrance—a passageway through a row of terraced houses into the old coach yard.

There is but one way out by road from Brightlingsea, past the splendid church which is sited so imposingly.

Cross Tenpenny Heath by moonlight, when the shadows are deep between the hedgerows and the waters of Alresford Creek glint beyond the trees. Drop silently into Wivenhoe and stand on the river's brink. Small rowing boats glide over the dark waters of the river, trailing wakes of silver. Diamonds sparkle on the oars. Now return up the High Street and enter the Falcon. The warm, friendly atmosphere is worlds away from the quiet mystery of the river. There is age here, but also a touch of today. At one end of the long bar some regulars play darts; at the other, when I was there, the interest was centred on a television performance of the ballet *Coppélia*!

The Falcon is as ancient as it looks. In the bar is displayed a token of about 1650 issued by John Parker at the Falken, Wivenhoe, if proof of age be needed. Again, in the registers of the church opposite are many ancient references.

For April 16, 1750:

" To a Vestry meeting at Falcon 12. 8
    Plume for beer (bier) in Gentry's illness and
      burial 6. 4
    Wm. Brown for liquor had to wkhouse etc. .. 3. 3. 3
    Parson and Clerk 3/6. Beer at burial 3/-.
      Nurses 3/- 1. 0. 6
    Mrs. Dunrell, ¼ Pint of Geneva 3
    ½ pint of wine for Cobb .. .. 4½ "

For 1757:

" A pint of wine to old Brown in his sickness .. 7
    Gin and ale at his burial 2. 6
    For a new shift for Dame Knock 5
    For an earthen dish, one soupladle, and 2
      chamberpots for Dame Knock 9
    Expenses of churchwarden at the inn .. .. 2. 0 "

Was the wine provided by the Falcon honestly come by? We wonder. And so did that scourge of the east coast smuggler the Wivenhoe-born Captain Harvey, skipper of the *Repulse*. Such an obstacle did this cutter become to the orderly passage of contraband to its inland destination that in 1780 the smugglers attempted to capture it. The attacking force consisted of four large cutters. One carried twenty-four six- and nine-pounders and the others nearly the same. They were to act in the double capacity of smugglers and privateers. They had French commissions and one Frenchman on board each to justify the taking of English prizes, although the rest of the crews were English and Irish. " They mean," says the contemporary report, " if they fall in with her to capture Captain Harvey's cutter, the *Repulse*, which is the object of the expedition."

Wivenhoe was not a healthy spot for smugglers towards the latter end of the eighteenth century, for besides Captain Harvey there was also a Captain Martin, who was equally ruthless in his pursuit of smugglers. Their combined efforts were not sufficient, however, to eradicate the lawbreakers. Opposition seems to whet the spirit of adventure in many people, acting as a challenge rather than a deterrent. The task of the smugglers was facilitated by the co-operation of most of the villagers, from policeman to parson.

One Wivenhoe tale illustrates this point. Two revenue officers requested the local policeman to accompany them to a house suspected of concealing brandy. Willingly he consented—until he saw the house under suspicion. Then he behaved like one demented. He rushed to the house shouting, " Take care of the pigs in your cherry garden."

This not very subtle warning confirmed the suspicions of the officers and they immediately tried forcing the front door. The constable attempted to stop them, threatening violence if they proceeded in their quest. Then he stood aside, an angry spectator. Having been forewarned about the character of the occupant of the house, the officers were reluctant to force an entry on their own, so they appealed once again for the constable's help. This proved a foolish request, for he behaved in the opposite manner, rushing at them, seizing them violently and threatening to " brain " them if they still persisted. Indeed, he stated with some heat that only regard for his position prevented his bashing out their brains there and then!

Constables did sometimes prove dependable, however, even more so than the churchwardens, according to the Rev. W. J. Hayes (author of *Wyvenhoe and Neighbourhood from the Earliest Times*, *Tennyson and Scientific Theology*, *Prehistoric Pottery*, and *Infant Care and Housecraft*). This versatile vicar points out in the first of the above books that one of the chief functions of the churchwardens was to leave the church after the second lesson in order to visit the public-houses and round up delinquents. The flesh was willing but the spirit proved too strong! They returned late and unsteady so often that eventually the bishop ordered that the constable should perform the task in their stead.

Of the many Wivenhoe smugglers one has become a legend. Sainty was the name. The story goes that when the Marquis of Anglesea wanted a new yacht with a fine turn of speed he was told that the best man to do the job was Sainty. At that moment Sainty was not occupied with his normal trade—he was resting in Chelmsford jail on a smuggling charge. He was interviewed. Of course he could build the yacht if the marquis could arrange his release. Yes, that could be arranged. And there were two of Sainty's relatives, also skilled yacht-builders, also serving sentences in Maidstone jail. If their release could be arranged that yacht would be built much quicker. Yes, that too could be arranged. The bargain was struck—the result, the famous *Pearl*.

Across the Colne from Wivenhoe lies Rowhedge, noted in days gone by for the ferocity of its sailors and fishermen. One notorious skipper seeing fingers grip the rail of his ship slashed at them first before inquiring about their owner. The Rowhedge men were wreckers as well as smugglers. When returning from spratting expeditions they encouraged ships of deeper draught to follow them over the sandbanks—with the inevitable result. All salvaged goods should have been delivered to the lighter which stood at the mouth of the Colne, but Rowhedge men ignored this formality. They preferred to land their loot behind the Pyefleet sea wall, hide it in the barns of willing farmers and then, when the coast was clear, distribute it to their many customers.

The manner in which they celebrated a successful coup was in keeping with their wild existence. No half measures for them! They assembled in the Three Crowns, placed a large bath in the centre of the floor, filled it with beer and scooped out their requirements with their quickly emptied tankards. And a good time was had by all . . .

Rowhedge is quiet enough these days, but Fingringhoe, lying beyond the Roman River, is even more peaceful. Its smallness does not prevent it from having a fine church and an interesting inn. The Whalebone was among the many Essex buildings damaged by the earthquake of 1884, but a successful " face-lift " has removed all signs of damage.

According to the landlady, the original sign was an actual whalebone. It was sent away for redecorating, but a wooden substitute was returned. This was sent back—and now, like the poor little dog, the inn has none.

In this pleasant inn of the old type there is no bar. The beer is kept in a cool cellar and served in a plain but cosy room, where in winter a coal fire burns in the unusual grate, made by the grandfather of the present blacksmith. Old meat hooks still hang in the chimney, while high in the corner of the room is a cage-like structure used formerly for storing hams and flitches.

A former landlord was a retired shipwright from Mersea called Spring Wycoll. His love of the river prompted him to design and construct an Emett-like creation—a punt motivated by the driving gear of a penny-farthing cycle. The machine worked, too, and the old man regularly journeyed to the Hythe in Colchester.

One stormy July day in 1782 an even stranger visitor arrived at the Hythe. The ship looked innocent enough, so did the chests which it deposited on the quay. But revenue officers, being what they are, eyed them with suspicion. The owner of the chests was a young Hamburg merchant named Mr. Williams. He knew no English, in spite of his name. The examination of the chests went smoothly. The lovely dresses and jewellery were quickly passed over—but when the officers started to examine the final chest Mr. Williams behaved like one possessed. He made it as clear as he could that it contained the body of his wife and nothing more. The officers had heard such tales before and took out their swords to test the contents by piercing. Mr. Williams became distraught and, drawing his own sword, threatened to kill anyone attempting to desecrate the chest. Naturally the revenue officers became even more suspicious and determined, but when at last they succeeded in opening the coffin they found that Mr. Williams had indeed been speaking the truth. Inside lay the embalmed body of a beautiful woman. The corpse was removed to the neighbouring church of St. Leonard, where the unhappy husband kept lone vigil for several nights.

Moved by the plight of the foreign gentleman, a local man with a knowledge of French endeavoured to console him. Mr. Williams appreciated the kindness and, bit by bit, unfolded his strange tale.

He was not a Hamburg merchant. His name was not Mr. Williams. He was, in fact, Lord Dalmeny, son of the Earl of Rosebery, and was born in Florence. Until about three years previously he had never visited England. On that occasion, while in London he had fallen in love with Kitty Cannon. They married, and soon after went abroad. Kitty's health, however, was not too good, and the travelling failed to improve it. Rapidly she got worse, and died. On her death-bed she confessed that she was already married when she met Lord Dalmeny, and that her first husband was still alive.

He was the Rev. Alexander Gough, rector of Thorpe-le-Soken. One thing she yearned for as slowly her strength ebbed away—to be borne back to Essex to be buried in the soil of her own parish. Lord Dalmeny promised to carry out her last request.

The ship set out for Harwich, but heavy weather forced it to find shelter in the Colne.

The strange tale was later confirmed by Kitty's first husband in language quite unclerical. However, the confirmation satisfied the revenue officers, who thereupon placed the strange but beautiful cargo in a decent coffin and had it conveyed to Thorpe-le-Soken. By this time Christian charity had soothed the savage breast of the Rev. Alexander Gough and we are left with a final picture—a fit ending to the tragic romance—of Alexander Gough and Lord Dalmeny walking side by side behind the coffin of the woman they both loved.

SCREEN   THORPE-LE-SOKEN

THE BLUE BOAR

CHAPTER IX

MEHALAH COUNTRY

FROM Fingringhoe we head for the Strood—that strange causeway anchoring Mersea Island to the mainland of Essex. Today we are in luck, for the waters of the Strood Channel and Pyefleet Creek are one, so the visit to Mersea City must be postponed a while until the ebb uncovers the causeway once more. A better place to await an ebb could hardly be found! Hard by the Strood is one of the loveliest inns in Essex, with the loveliest name— the Peldon Rose. The old house stands at the fork made by the junction of the roads from Colchester and Maldon.

The inn is entered through an arch of roses, and once inside you are back in the days of the smugglers of yesteryear. But today and every day the talk is not of hollands, silk or baccy, but of wildfowl. As the last night of September approaches the conversation becomes more and more animated, and the thought of the chill vigil in low punts down in the cold creeks calls for a nip of something to warm the marrow in advance.

Outside the Rose the innocent-looking pond, now the home of carolinas, mandarins and other musically named ducks, was at one time a favourite repository for contraband. The kegs were sunk with stones, then covered with a layer of soil to hoodwink the revenue officers into believing that the bottom was level. At other times blocks of salt were used to sink the barrels. Some days later the salt dissolved and the barrels floated to the top, where they were collected by a watchful smuggler.

The tide has ebbed and the Strood is clear. The road across it continues to East Mersea, but beyond the Dog and Pheasant peters out into marshland and saltings.

A name for ever linked with this region is that of S. Baring-Gould. He was rector of East Mersea for ten years, from 1871 to 1881. " I cannot say that I ever liked the place or became attached

57

to the people," he wrote in his *Early Reminiscences*, but in spite of this feeling he left us in his novel *Mehalah* a vivid picture of both people and place as they were in the late nineteenth century.

This tale deserves to be better known. It has been compared with *Lorna Doone*, and certainly it does for Essex what Blackmore's book does for Devon. Against the wild backcloth of the lonely, wind-swept marshes is enacted the terrifying love drama of Elijah Rebow and the beautiful Mehalah. Of the many characters in the book, she only possessed any goodness or nobility of character. All else were drunkards, liars, cheats and worse. Elijah himself was the quintessence of evil. In him were concentrated all the vices of the marshmen. His one admirable trait was his constancy to Mehalah. To this we should add his perfect command of the English language. This uniformly high standard of speech of all the characters in *Mehalah* is, perhaps, its chief weakness. A sample of Elijah's conversation illustrates the point:

" Whilst we are on earth we cannot be united, because he [Rebow's rival] intercepts the current which runs from my heart to yours, and yours to mine. Although he might be far away, a thousand miles distant, yet the tide of your affection would set to him. The moon, they tell us, is some hundreds of thousands of miles from the ocean, and yet the water throbs and rises, and falls and retreats responsive to the impulse of the moon, because the moon and earth are both in one sphere. As long as you and he are together in one orb, there is no place for me, your love will never flow to me and dance and sparkle about me."

Baring-Gould was well acquainted with the smuggling habits of his parishioners. One of the old smugglers' haunts in West Mersea, the White Hart, is still an inn, but the other, the Old Victory, is now peacefully serving as two cottages. Near the church is a house called Orleans which still retains a smuggler's lookout. This square structure with a pyramidal roof surmounts the stable. The view it commands is considerable—from the mouth of the Colne in a great sweep out to sea and up the Blackwater as far as Osea Island.

Mersea City has changed considerably since the days of Baring-Gould, but little imagination is required to picture the town as it was 100 years ago. Remove, in your mind's eye, the recent buildings and picture a lonely, windswept island with only a few half-timbered cottages huddled around the church. In these lived the hard men wresting an existence from the land, the sea and the air. In season they hunted wildfowl, lying throughout the bitterly cold night in their low grey punts, contracting both ague and rheumatism. Can it be wondered at, then, that they regarded smuggling as an easy way of supplementing their meagre existence? And woe betide anyone who dared to interfere! Baring-Gould wrote that a boat's crew of excisemen, twenty-two in number, were once found off Sunken Island with their throats cut. Their bodies were taken to Salcott churchyard, where they were buried, with their boat turned keel uppermost over their graves. But there was one occasion when the men of Salcott were themselves taken by surprise. One night when, for a change, they were sleeping peacefully in their beds, a boat crept stealthily up the creek and a small body of men landed near the church. Entering the building, they ascended the tower, removed the bells and bore them off to Holland.

The road to Maldon takes us through a countryside ringing with knightly Norman names—Tolleshunt D'Arcy, Tolleshunt Major, Layer-de-la-Haye. This too is Mehalah country, and the twin hamlets of Salcott and Virley figure prominently in the book. It was at the Sun inn, Salcott, that Mehalah sought work after fleeing the ardent attentions of Rebow. The present inn is modern but is built on the site of the original building, which was of one story only. The old Hall can be reached by going to the end of the lane and walking in the direction of Tollesbury.

Across the bridge from Salcott is Virley, and it was in the church of that hamlet that the fantastic wedding of Mehalah and Rebow took place. The church is now a ruin, but both chancel and nave can still be distinguished. The ruin is not without charm. In the spring, primroses, daffodils and wallflowers grow at the foot of the ivy-clad walls—a picture of peace. How different from those days when the congregation consisted largely of local smugglers, who attended, said Baring-Gould, not to pay homage to God but to keep an eye on their contraband concealed in various parts of the church. This church was dedicated to St. Mary, but " who among the holy ones would spread his mantle over worshippers who were smugglers or wreckers?" To ease their consciences the smugglers had erased the " nots " from the copy of the Decalogue displayed in the church.

Near St. Mary's stood the White Hart, now also a ruin, but once well known as a smugglers' haunt. Looking back across the creek, the string of buildings that is Salcott presents an unusual sight, and it is not difficult to picture the place as it was 100 or so years ago when the populations of both villages were " engaged in the contraband trade. Every house had its shed and stable, where was a donkey and cart, to be let on occasions to carry smuggled goods inland."

" Inland " was probably Tiptree Heath, which was used as a kind of clearing house by the smugglers of this region of Essex. The contraband was hidden in underground chambers cunningly concealed with vegetation, and remained there until it was safe to distribute it farther afield.

The smugglers' organization was rough and ready, but seems to have been effective. A signal from an elevated position—a hill or church tower for example—could be seen for miles in this region, which is scarcely anywhere much above sea level. A light flashed on Tiptree Heath could be picked up by men of Virley, who in turn could signal to watchers on Beacon Hill, right across the Crouch near St. Lawrence.

Tolleshunt D'Arcy looks well groomed after Salcott, doing credit to its aristocratic name. The modern Red Lion and the older Queen's Head and Thatchers' Arms are all in keeping with the atmosphere of the village.

The lonely road winds on to Maldon, passing, in Heybridge, the Wave, aptly named by a retired sea-captain who was responsible for converting the former house into the present inn.

Maldon has many inns of interest, but the one which is justly noteworthy is the Blue Boar. This name might indicate that the house at one time belonged to the de Veres, since that was their favourite badge. Their ancestral home was only about twenty miles away in Hedingham. The last of the earls dismantled the castle in the seventeenth century and it is believed that one of his retainers was given the Maldon house, which he converted into an inn under the badge of his former master.

To obtain an idea of the age of the inn it is better to approach it from the rear. At right-angles to the front of the inn is a fifteenth-century building, half-timbered and with a beetling upper story surmounted by a high-pitched tiled roof. The smallish coachyard narrows to the archway, which leads to the street and the church of All Saints beyond. We glimpse the spire above the roof and remember that Lawrence Washington, great-grandfather of George, was buried in All Saints in 1652. Viewed from the church the façade of the Blue Boar is seen to be unspectacular eighteenth-century apart from the not unpleasant Georgian porch.

Behind this eighteenth-century front are two late-fifteenth-century rooms, one panelled in Jacobean oak, some panels being *in situ*. Above these, the one-time assembly hall is divided up into bedrooms. Its former antechamber is now a drawing room with a white mantelpiece of the eighteenth century.

In the old wing the bar and tea room have high ceilings supported by wide oak beams, and in the billiard room above are more beams and a great king-post.

The Blue Boar depends upon its architectural features rather than on its association for its attraction. We cannot be certain if the inn was a coaching house, in spite of its appearance. And was this the place meant by the Water Poet when he wrote of a " taverne for a safe harbour kept or allowed by Ursula Edwards "? We cannot be sure.

" Harbour " is a happy choice of word when talking about Maldon's inns, for here we have a fishing town where the bar-talk is of tides, of ships, of the weather and of fish. To savour the salt-tang of this talk you should drop into the Jolly Sailor or the Queen's Head—inns which can be said to have their feet in the river. The boat-builders and river-men yarn away the hours, enjoying the warm evening peace of the homely bars as only men accustomed to the long, hard hours on the cruel sea know how.

Maldon has a King's Head as well as a Queen's Head. It is referred to in the chamberlain's accounts for 1624: "And of the 16s. payd to Jasper Kingsman the younger for the dynners of twenty and fower souldyers, imprested for the towne at the inne called the King's Head, and of 22d for firewood and beere spent by them before dynner."

The " twenty and fower " later found themselves overseas fighting for the son-in-law of James I, Frederick of the Palatinate.

In the State Papers for 1586 is a petition which suggests that methods of becoming a publican are varied and many. One Jane Stantie was regarded by many as a prophetess. In order to fulfil one of her wilder forecasts a certain Mantell agreed to impersonate the dead king, Edward VI. Elizabeth Vessie and Thomas Collins discovered the plot and Mantell was tried and convicted. He managed to escape and cheat the executioners.

For the "discovery of Mr. Mantell the Traitor," Collins petitioned for a reward. Being of a generous nature, he himself suggested numerous alternatives to the authorities. He was willing to accept a twenty-one-year licence as a free victualler, a licence to transport 400 tins of beer, or failing these a gratuity of £40 cash.

A book dealing with inns is hardly a fit place to discuss temperance. The reader might even find it stranger to associate the name of Charrington with the same subject, but looking at that low, empty island in the river—Osea—recalls a strange aberration in the family of the celebrated brewers.

Frederick Nicholas Charrington was standing outside one of his family's public-houses in the East End of London when he saw a woman, with young children clinging to her skirts, beg money from her drunken husband so that she could buy food for the children. All she got was a fist in the face.

"It knocked her into the gutter and me out of the brewery," wrote Frederick. Soon after he sold his brewery shares for £1,000,000, and this he spent on his temperance campaigns.

One of his enterprises was to establish on Osea "a house for gentlemen suffering from the baneful and insidious effects of alcohol." There was to be no public-house on the island, but unfortunately for the alcoholics anonymous the local boatmen undermined their moral resolve by smuggling strong drink to the publess plot! Charrington arranged for the minds of the men attempting to escape from pink elephants to be filled by the unusual spectacle of imported kangaroos, emus, cockatoos and seals. One can imagine some strange complexes developing in minds already struggling against the torture of excessive alcohol!

The worthy enterprise did not last long, and Osea is once again a quiet, undistinguished island.

Some miles from Maldon is Danbury, standing on a hill commanding an extensive view. Little wonder that the summit was used as a fort by Saxons, Romans and others. For the last 200 years the Griffin's Head has attracted rather than repelled invaders. Actually it is twice that age, but it is doubtful if it has been an inn throughout its existence. The first known reference occurs in 1750. It is not mentioned in 1733 when the local bellringers supped alternately at the Blue Boar and the Star throughout that year.

The interior of the Griffin's Head is warm and cosy. Dark oak beams which were once ships' timbers support the roof and some carved woodwork of the fifteenth century is said to have come from the church during the Reformation. Two imposing chairs are said to have belonged to the bishop's palace at Danbury. Upstairs some wall-stencilling suggests that the artist who decorated the north aisle of the church was also employed by the Griffin's Head landlord. Perhaps he paid his bill in this manner ! Over the bedroom in the south-west corner of the house is a secret chamber, so it is said, approached only through the chimney.

Hanging on the wall downstairs between reproductions of resplendent M.O.H.s is a will, partly burned, which was found after an air raid in 1940. It states that in 1789 Thomas Bacon, victualler and inn-holder of Danbury, left £30 to his son William Cooper, of Little Baddow ; £10 to his son Abraham, of Braintree ; and £130 to his natural daughter, Mary Butcher. The cattle, furniture, etc., were to be shared equally among them. The signature and the names of the witnesses appear to have been cut off deliberately. Is it so surprising ?

One is rather surprised, however, to find a connection between Danbury and Sir Walter Scott. It came about in this way. The antiquary Joseph Strutt had left a novel unfinished when he died. It was *Queenhoo Hall*. Many of the scenes are laid at Danbury, at Gay Bowers in the castle of the St. Clere family, which stood near the manor house. Scott's publishers thought that the novel had some merit, so they asked him to write the last two chapters. This he did, completing the book in 1808, six years after the death of Strutt.

Scott had been working on *Waverley* just before this commission. What he had written did not please him, so he placed the book to one side and forgot about it. Some time later he rediscovered the manuscript when sorting out some material and, recalling the success of *Queenhoo Hall*, decided to publish *Waverley*. The book appeared in 1814.

In 1902, Father Ignatius, of Llanthony Abbey, that fiery and eccentric prelate, stayed in the inn.

Near Danbury are two inns well worth visiting—the Anchor at Runsell Green for its cosy interior and the Bell at Woodham Walter for its Elizabethan exterior. What a delightful surprise to drop down past the Elizabethan church to find such a large, attractive period piece set in a picturesque hollow. The general effect is impressive and closer examination of the structure reveals, on the overhanging story, tendrils of the vine, oak leaves and acorns carved in the old oak timbers. In the public bar the true Essex accent can be heard. It can also be heard in the Anchor. This building, just off the main Brentwood road, cannot be missed—and should not!—for hanging against the white walls are a huge anchor and a ship's wheel. The interior is warm and inviting, with brick, black timbers, carved settles and a wealth of brass all pleasantly blending. If you are lucky enough to be there when the beams from the westering sun shine through the bottle-glass windows to cast strange patterns on the dark woodwork and the sparkling glasses and bottles you will certainly want to return to enjoy a drink in the delightful bar.

THE BELL
WOODHAM MORTIMER

BLUE BOAR
MALDON

THE GRIFFIN
· DANBURY ·

THE GREEN MAN
BRADWELL on SEA

STAR HOTEL
BURNHAM on CROUCH

CHAPTER X

BRADWELL AND BURNHAM

BETWEEN the Blackwater and the Crouch is a region as lonely as any part of Essex. Most of the inhabitants are to be found in half a dozen townships, the largest being Burnham-on-Crouch. It is hardly the place then to find famous inns. Smallish public-houses are more in keeping with the country-side. At Southminster the railway ends and two inns record the fact in their names, and how oddly they sound in this land which, one feels, should not have heard of railways but only of foot travellers, horses and boats. In the bars of the inns of Southminster, Dengie and Asheldam the clear-eyed men, slightly bent but with shoulders grown big from steadying the plough, talk slowly of the weather, of the crops, of the fields and woods. But in Bradwell-juxta-Mare—or plain Brad'll to the East Saxon—we hear of the sea and of boats, besides the weather. The Green Man, standing on the waterfront, is naturally a favourite rendezvous of seafaring types, and how refreshing is their talk! We landlubbers tend to regard the sea as an extension, unpleasantly wet, of the land. But the sea-going man regards the land as an appendage to the sea. Archie White's book *Tideways and Byways in Essex and Suffolk* illustrates this second viewpoint. For instance:

" At the quay there is good clean landing at all states of the tide, and one soon discovers the Green Man. Many yachtsmen discover it immediately on rounding the bend in the creek, for it stands out boldly on the side of the road with a field before it sloping to the water's edge. These enthusiasts fasten their eyes upon the inn, keeping their bowsprits generally in its direction. Some keep a certain chimney in line with a bush in the foreground. Others make no bones about it, but steer for the open door, running aground before reaching it."

We landsmen approaching from the dry side step from the

street straight into a bar parlour and notice at once the huge elm table lining one wall. This, we are told, was used as a workbench about forty years ago by a landlord who made coffins for his former customers between pulling pints for his customers—present and future. He was a man of many occupations—innkeeper, pigkeeper, coal merchant and undertaker. Over the huge fire-grate he always kept a cauldron of potatoes hanging from the hook so that visiting bargemen might help themselves to something much more warming and filling than the present-day bag of crisps.

Above the 500-year-old fireplace in the bar is a board with the strange inscription:

> " MORE SHALL TRUST SCORE I SENT
> FOR WHAT I MY AND HAS
> DO BEER IF PAY CLERK BREWER
> I MY AND MUST HIS THE."

To solve this double talk begin with the last word and read upwards.

A former Bradwell inn was called The Case is Altered. The sign was not unique, there being a number in different parts of the country, each with a local interpretation of the meaning. Perhaps the most widespread explanation is that which tells of the new landlord who commemorated his advent by abolishing the " slate." Another recalls the incident of the farmer and the great lawyer Plowden.

" My bull has gored and killed your cow," said the farmer.

" Well," said the lawyer, " the case is clear; you must pay me her value."

" Oh," said the farmer, " I have made a mistake. It is your bull which has killed my cow."

" Ah! the case is altered," quoth Plowden.

Near the church is the tiny village lock-up, a feature found in most villages up to 1840. I hardly think it was much used in Bradwell, certainly not when Hezekiah Staines was constable. It was common knowledge that he actively assisted the local smugglers. A favourite hiding place for contraband was the Saxon church which stands gaunt and lonely by the sea. It was a brave revenue officer who would approach the building of a night time across the deserted fields when the biting wind howled in from the North Sea. No wonder that smuggling was profitable along these coasts. One muggler, Captain Wegg by name, amassed sufficient money to retire to Jaywick, near Clacton, where he had a house built for himself. Years later, when this same house was pulled down, a secret room was found beneath the kitchen. So it seems that even in retirement the captain did not sever all connections with his former occupation.

In Clacton, too, another discovery was made when a house called Treasure Holt was demolished in 1928. Beneath the floor of the living room were found a number of bones, a shoe buckle and a token inscribed *John Wilkins, Ironmaster 1793*. It has been surmised that the unfortunate ironmaster had discovered a gang of smugglers celebrating a successful run and that death had been his reward.

In our pursuit of inns it is difficult to avoid smugglers, and before our story is ended we shall encounter many more. They are seldom far from our thoughts as we wander through the lonely Essex byways towards Burnham-on-Crouch. Now and then a lane or path runs off our route leading to nowhere in particular, frequently petering out in the marshes and saltings of Dengie and Tillingham.

Is there another place just like Burnham? Who can wander along that winding walk that follows the water-front—past the old inns, the yachts in the making in the shipyards, the superannuated yachts tied securely to the river wall, the yachts sleek and trim ready for the water—and not be thrilled? Even if you have as little nautical knowledge as myself, not knowing a poop from a scupper!

Mix with the clientele of the White Hart or the Star and again you are made to understand that beyond the shore-line there exists another world but dimly realized by the landsman. The duffle coats, sweaters and thigh-boots of Bradwell's Green Man are absent from the lounges of Burnham's hotels, but the talk is still of the sea. And what a backcloth the river provides for such conversation—the river glimpsed through the windows. Tales of fair weather, of storms, tales told by yachtsmen famous and infamous. Wash the salt from your lips with a tankard of the best and talk, talk . . . But alas, all these tales go unrecorded.

Hynes the buccaneer could have told stories of his life which would have dimmed the best heard today in the White Hart. Of course, when he visited the place the present respectability was

completely lacking, Burnham being but a small fishing village in
a remote part of Essex. He ended his days overlooking the river—
the Thames, not the Crouch. He was executed, then hanged in
chains with two other criminals at Fiddler's Point, Greenhithe.
This gruesome sight was intended to act as an awful warning to
pirates, night-plunderers, scuffle-hunters, mud-larks, light-horse-
men, heavy-horsemen and other shady characters who haunted the
river.

Westward from Burnham the road runs just high enough to
provide us with glimpses of the Crouch and those famous hills
beyond which are written indelibly into the nation's story—the
hills where Canute defeated the English.

The WHITE HART
BURNHAM on CROUCH

CHAPTER XI

REVENUE LAWS AND OFFICERS FOR EVER

WE cross the river at Battlesbridge, standing at the head of the tidal Crouch, to find a weatherboarded inn with the appropriate sign of the Barge. Down river about two miles, at Hullbridge, are the Anchor and the Smuggler's Den. Both occupy fine sites, but from the former nothing of the river can be seen through its large windows. Nothing can be seen of the lovely sunsets which touch with magic the rather drab banks of the river—a fine opportunity missed! During the war the Anchor had close connections with the French Maquis, not maritime as one might think, but aerial, and some of these aerial connections can still be seen flying around the inn or in their cotes! These pigeons, if you have not guessed, were placed in cardboard boxes and dropped by parachute at a time and place arranged, where a reception committee affixed a small papier-mâché container to the legs of each bird and released them immediately. When the pigeons arrived back at Hullbridge, the landlord of the Anchor removed the message and, without opening it, placed it in a special envelope, which he handed to the guard of the first train to leave Rayleigh for London. At Liverpool Street station the same guard handed it to a waiting dispatch rider, who delivered it to British Intelligence.

All the birds did not return home. Some were killed, others were captured by the Germans, who replaced the message by a charge which exploded when the receiver opened it.

The Smuggler's Den is a much older building than the Anchor, but its ancient interior is reserved nowadays for club members only.

Disentangle yourself from the mess of cottages that is Hullbridge and it is pleasant to wander around the leafy lanes of the Rochford hundred. Go by way of Hockley and you will no doubt be struck by the Spa hotel. It was constructed in the mid-nineteenth century to house patients who had come to take the waters at the local spa. The venture was not a great success, and the proprietor was forced to the conclusion that his customers had more faith in beer than in medicinal waters.

The alleged efficacy of these waters was discovered about 183 by Robert Clay and his wife Letitia. The latter lost her persistent cough when she moved from Cheltenham to Hockley. Naturally being a lady from Gloucester, she thought in terms of " waters, although Benton the Essex historian suggested that the change of air had worked the cure. Anyway, the proprietor of the well, a London solicitor named Fawcett, thought that there were possibilities and sent a sample of the water to be analysed. A Dr Granville who saw the report asserted that the chemical content of the water should be efficacious in complaints of the rickety variety, and for dyspepsia.

Fawcett was now convinced that a spa could be developed, so he built the pump room in 1842 and the hotel a few years later. The spa failed to attract the anticipated invalids and the solicitor lost money. The buildings are now a memorial to his good intentions. The hotel is still an hotel, but the pump room was, not inappropriately, a Baptist chapel for a time, but is now a shirt factory.

The spa had some devoted believers in its efficacy. One person of note in the Rochford hundred used to send his servant regularly for supplies and benefited considerably from drinking them. It was much later that he learned that the water he had been taking was not the Hockley water at all, but merely that obtained from a local spring. It seems that the servant disliked the long walk to Hockley, so he got his supplies from the spring, then spent the rest of his time taking anything but water in the Battlesbridge Hawk.

Benton, whose scholarly book on the Rochford hundred is such a mine of information, recounts a " heathenish baptism " at Canewdon. Before the tenor bell was hung in the church tower, the workmen carried it to the Anchor, filled it with beer and " partook of copious libations."

Beyond Canewdon we encounter again those Essex lanes that lead to nowhere in particular, so it is unwise to travel without a good map. One's wanderings are further complicated by a maze of waterways—pools, reaches, creeks, swatchways and fleets dividing the flats into a watery mosaic, a land and sea pattern designed for smugglers! And we are not disappointed. **Paglesham** looks innocent enough today, but when Blyth was the " king of the smugglers " the hamlet was a place to be avoided. Hard Apple, to give him his other alias, was a remarkable character. In " civil " life he was village grocer and churchwarden, occupations not unrelated, since he used to tear out pages from the parish record books to use as wrappings for his butter and cheese.

Many a good tale is told of Hard Apple. He could drink anyone under the table of the Punch Bowl, the inn that stood near the church on the village green. It was in this inn too that he not only drank two glasses of wine but ate the glasses as well. No ill effect is recorded.

His toughness was a byword. Between escapades he and his fellow travellers liked nothing better than a game of cricket on the village green. It was their custom to remove their coats and place them on the grass within easy reach, with their guns on top—not to shoot the umpire, but in case of sudden interruptions from foreigners, as law officers were called. They were alarmed on one occasion, not by the revenue officers but by a bull that came charging on to the field. " Body and bones! " yelled Blyth. " Don't think to frighten me! " Straightway he grabbed the bull by the tail with one hand and belaboured the creature with the home-made cricket bat which he held in the other. This unexpected turn of events, man attacking bull, so alarmed the animal that it retreated at full speed but dropped exhausted from a mixture of fright, pommelling and unwonted exercise.

On one of his smuggling runs Blyth's ship was captured by the law officers. Always resourceful, he readily agreed to the transference of the contraband to the government ship. While this was taking place Blyth got on good terms with the officers and soon the grog began to flow. When the officers were sufficiently fuddled the contraband was moved in the opposite direction. The task completed to Blyth's satisfaction, officers and smugglers parted on the best of terms.

Blyth was captured on another occasion off the French coast and clamped in irons below deck. On the home run the government schooner got stuck on the Dogger Bank and all the efforts of her crew failed to dislodge her. Swallowing his pride, the captain appealed to Blyth to help him, for the smuggler's skill as a sailor was well known. He was deaf to the appeal. Why should he help?

Might as well be drowned as hanged! Further efforts to dislodge the ship were unavailing, so again the captain implored Blyth to help him. This time he softened. He saved the ship and lived to smuggle another day.

He died in 1820. On his death-bed he sent for a Mr. Page, of Church-Hall, and asked him to read aloud a particular chapter from the Bible, then to repeat the Lord's Prayer. Page did as he was asked, then Blyth said " Now I am ready for the launch," closed his eyes and died.

Blyth's father-in-law was John Dowsett. He too was a notorious smuggler renowned for his daring. He equipped a cutter called *Big Jane* with six brass six-pounders and his encounters with the revenue officers were fought with great ferocity as a consequence.

Some pollarded elms growing near Pound Pond near East Hall were favourite places for hiding the contraband. According to Benton it was not unusual for £200 worth of silk to be concealed in them at one time. The total amount of contraband brought into the Paglesham district was enormous. Wool was the chief import and the quantity can be judged when it is realized that the annual illegal import of geneva and brandy exceeded 13,000 gallons. Most of the contraband was temporarily concealed on the lonely island of Yantlet, lying off the Kentish coast, until such time as the smugglers had a clear run to the Essex shore. Once this was reached they were assisted by the fact that it was possible to travel from the Thames to the Crouch by the maze of waterways joining the two rivers—and it was a brave revenue man who dared to follow!

Much of the information concerning smugglers and smuggling in this area is to be found in John Harriott's book *Struggles Through Life*. He lived in Great Stambridge and his importance lies in the fact that he was instrumental in forming the Thames river police.

On one occasion he wanted to return to England from Dunkirk. In a tavern in that town he fell in with some smugglers from Kent and soon arranged a passage for home. The smugglers proposed a toast to " the damnation of all revenue officers." Harriott objected and brought curses on his head for doing so. Being a man of some character, he maintained that he was right and they were wrong. He argued that if the revenue officers were abolished there would then be no smugglers; they would become merely common traders.

" Would you then be as well off as you are now? " " Lost," said the chairman, " so here goes: Revenue laws and officers for ever! "

Harriott sailed at midnight and landed within half a mile of his house.

To explore the inns south of the river we pass through Rochford, standing at the head of the River Roach. Here even the church was used by the smugglers, no doubt with the parson's consent. Gin, hollands and quantities of tea were all concealed in the tower, and a cavity underneath the pulpit was called the magazine.

Rochford was of some importance when Southend was South End, a mere village, and consequently it has some of the oldest and most interesting inns in the Rochford hundred. The Old Ship—there is also a New Ship—is renowned because the last men to be hanged for sheep stealing were connected with it. They were Thomas Fairhead and Henry Gilliott. The former kept a butcher's stall in the yard of the inn where he lodged; the latter was a shepherd for Thomas Laver at Prittlewell Temple, where the offence was committed. Fairhead was engaged to Mary Water, daughter of the Old Ship's landlord, and she, poor girl, died of a broken heart. The men were hanged in Moulsham old jail on March 24, 1820. Not so long ago!

Another Rochford inn worth visiting for its architecture alone is the Marlborough Head. It is an ancient building and, in the evenings when the lights shine warmly through its leaded windows, quite irresistible. Rumour has it that Wellington billeted his officers in the inn, but no evidence is put forward to support this claim. The fact that the inn and several neighbouring buildings are interconnected might have suggested a barracks, and the name of the inn itself, by some twist of reasoning, might have lent support to the claim. Left of the entrance doorway is a small room where marketing farmers were wont to drink in days gone by. It was their custom to bring a hen and eggs into the room with them and to leave only when the chicks left the eggs. A novel excuse!

Overlooking the old market place is the King's Head. In March 1955 a number of prominent citizens sat down to a dinner consisting of boiled leg of mutton, roast joints, apple pie, caper sauce, plum pudding and best beer. This sumptuous meal was a revival of a ceremony that had persisted for centuries but had died out about 100 years ago. Reading the menu once again makes me wonder why the ceremony was so long in being revived!

When the dinner was ended, the participants proceeded to an old house called King's Hill in Stambridge Road. On the lawn of this house they stood in a circle around a square pole about three feet high just as other citizens had done 300 years before.

When this practice began no one knows, but the story goes that a certain Earl of Warwick returned home unexpectedly from foreign wars. At midnight he was awakened by the crowing of cocks, and, hearing some confused murmurings outside his window, proceeded quietly across the room. He discovered that certain of his tenants, obviously unaware of his return, were plotting to kill him when he returned from overseas. He recognized the plotters and inflicted a unique penalty on them—they and their descendants were to assemble at midnight once every year and answer to a roll call.

This Great Lawless Court or Whispering Court was formerly held in Rayleigh until its transference to Rochford by the second Earl of Warwick, who died in 1658. The court itself is unique, and in the course of centuries many unusual practices became associated with it. The meal eaten in 1955 was more or less traditional, but one heart-and-body-warming feature was omitted—the sweet punch. This was made in a large bowl and served with a silver ladle containing a coin of the reign of George II. The steaming brew was made of rum, brandy, port, sherry, shrub spruce, hot water, lemon and much sugar. Following the loyal toast songs were sung, varying quantities of the punch were drunk and a good time was had by all—with the possible exception of the chairman, who had to remain more or less sober, for it was his duty to notify the approach of midnight and listen for the crowing of the cock.

At the stroke of midnight the chairman stood up, then led the way to the whispering post. Noisy youths accompanied the procession, crowing like cocks all the way. Arriving at the post the tenants knelt in a circle and the chairman, after the traditional oyez in triplicate, called out names, one by one, from his roll. If the tenant was present his name was ticked off with a piece of charcoal. When the list was duly checked the tenants dispersed, making their separate, but purposeful, ways to the King's Head, where, wrote Benton, " if licence has been obtained, another bowl of punch is indulged in, the guests quitting at one in the morning."

This age-old custom finally deteriorated into a drunken, rowdy gathering and its suppression was inevitable.

When three Welshmen meet the result is an eisteddfod. When three Englishmen meet the result is a party. This can be concluded from the doings at the King's Head, and if further evidence is necessary one has only to open a parish account book. Barling is south of the Roach and east of Rochford. Formerly it was the custom of the churchwardens and overseers of this village to regale themselves with ale at the expense of the community, for after all, they probably reasoned, they were engaged on parish work! Little could be said when the annual outlay on ale was 1/6, but an examination of the accounts of the parish meetings towards the end of the eighteenth century shows an alarming increase in expenditure and in the variety of beverages consumed. Beer, brandy, hollands and genevas must have made the meetings sound like an old-time music hall. In fairness to the officers, however, it must be stated that all the parish money was not spent on drink. Some was spent on veal, mutton and other " nescarys." And what session would be complete without pipes and tobacco?—on the parish, of course, to the tune of £40 in the year 1725.

The neighbouring town of Great Wakering—climatically the driest spot in the British Isles—was, in the early nineteenth century, notorious for its Sunday drunkenness and general rowdiness. This was not entirely due to the inhabitants, but to the great number of wanted criminals who, endeavouring to escape the penalties of their crimes, attempted to lose their identities in the loneliness of this region.

Nowadays the little town is quiet enough, and most sober. Its main street is pleasant; the whitewashed brick exterior of the Exhibition inn gives it the air of a demure nun. The sign of the Skylon—the symbol of the 1951 exhibition—should not be allowed to mislead you into mistaking the age of the inn. Step inside the door of the saloon and huge engravings of the 1851 exhibition remind you of the earlier Victorian affair. Has one entered a museum? No; the bottles on the bar shelves reassure us. All around are objects as different as a candlestick set in gimbals and a monastery bell, but overall the bar has a distinct nautical flavour. We sit in tub chairs from H.M.S. *Ganges* (the last seagoing flagship under sail) at a table with a glass top supported by a wheel from an old sailing ship, and are watched by the great eyes of a moose which once decorated the wardroom of H.M.S. *Hood*, which was stripped, you may remember, to chase the *Bismarck*. The other objects are too numerous and too diverse to describe or even to list, but the various weapons of offence and the offensive-looking weapons are worth noticing. So too are the water clock made by Curtis in Salisbury in 1691; the Chinese temple drum; the two-headed toby jug; the brass trays—and if you like the gruesome there is always the pickled freak dog or the mongoose entwined by two snakes.

The saloon bar is the one usually patronized by curious visitors. If, however, you want to savour local colour the public bar is the one for you. True, there are numerous objects to gaze at—the usual wealth of brass ornaments, instruments of torture, swords, daggers, boomerangs, axes, musical bells—but the most interesting features of the room are the people. Listen quietly. Those weatherbeaten men with navy-blue polo-necked sweaters talk easily of tides and winds and catches; in the other corner a lively band of slow-talking characters discusses crops and cattle, reminisces about the old days before roads in these parts were surfaced, recalls those long treks to markets and suddenly explodes with laughter at a ribald anecdote concerning Rayner's mare. And so it goes on—whiffs of the sea mingle with wafts from the farmyard, for this delightful little village of Great Wakering is like so many other Essex villages—amphibious.

Great Wakering used to be lonely, but the neighbouring island of Foulness was even lonelier and certainly more primitive. At one time, in fact, the supply of water was almost non-existent. What little there was was kept under lock and key. This shortage led to a strange reversal in the value of hollands and water. The former was freely given to the island's visitors, but the latter was valuable enough to smuggle!

In a region as lonely as Foulness Island, and where many of the men were "on the run," it was to be expected that fist-fighting was a fairly common practice. The churchyard was the favourite battle-ground, not because the loser could be more easily interred, but because it was next door to the inn. The hard-drinking toughs settled any argument started in the pub by stepping directly into the churchyard, there being no wall in those days.

According to Benton, Turtle's Wall, a highway from Ringwood to the church, was so called in the eighteenth century to commemorate a fierce fight in which one of the contestants was killed.

Probably the greatest fighter produced on the island was John

Bennewith. From 1810 he was acknowledged to be the Foulness champion. Men with such awe-inspiring names as the Giant and Bullock's Bone bowed before his might, which was not inconsiderable when it is recalled that he frequently disposed of his challengers when fighting with one hand only.

His most memorable fight was with a professional London pugilist called Leggatt, who happened to be in the district working as a plasterer in Southminster church. When Bennewith entered the ring he shook hands with Leggatt, then commenced to sing a ballad written specially for the occasion—a practice indulged in of late years by some Irish fighters. Whether the idea was to entertain the spectators or to terrify the opponent has not been made clear. If the latter, then Bennewith's efforts were unavailing, for he was struck down several times and looked a defeated man. At this point his wife, who was acting with his brother as a second, said some very unfriendly things to him. What they were we do not know, but there can be no doubt as to their efficacy. Bennewith charged into the fray with renewed vigour and punched Leggatt so hard that he sustained several fractured ribs. The fight was over.

To celebrate the occasion, the victor led the way to the King's Head, Southminster, where he danced a victory " hornpipe in the happiest style—being one of the best dancers of his class."

PUNCH BOWL
PAGLESHAM

CHAPTER XII

INNS OF THE SEA REACH

AN inn situated on the banks of the Thames is worthy of a visit even if it has no tale to tell or striking architecture to claim our attention. The mere fact that it stands near the bank of one of the great rivers of the world is in itself sufficient recommendation. To sit on the wall of the Peter Boat at Leigh, or on the veranda of Purfleet's Royal Hotel, and watch the ships go by is a delight hard to surpass. All the romance of the world is in those ships. The artist in us admires their beauty; the poet in us climbs on board to be borne to the far corners of the world.

Enter the mouth of the Thames and Southend pier comes out to greet you. Follow it to its landward end and you arrive at the hotels standing prominently on the former cliff-tops.

The Royal hotel was built in 1791 at the same time as Royal Terrace. From White's gazetteer we learn that the Royal was "an extensive and commodious building with elegant assembly and coffee rooms, standing at the east end of the Terrace in full view of the Thames, the pier and the ocean." We learn from the same source that one daily coach left for London at the remarkable hour of four in the morning and another at the more reasonable time of 9 a.m. The route led through Rochford, Rayleigh, Billericay and on to the Blue Boar, Aldgate.

The hotel and the Terrace derive their names from Princess Caroline of Wales, wife of the Prince Regent, who in 1803 stayed in numbers 7 and 8 of the Terrace. She acted somewhat foolishly and her lax behaviour resulted in a commission of investigation. This was really prompted by the wild statements of one Robert Bidgood, who swore that a Captain Manby had slept in the same house and even in the same bedroom as the princess. His evidence was entirely circumstantial, as the commissioners showed, but they did add that the princess had behaved with a general levity unbecoming in one of her rank.

Later, in 1868, another royal visitor came to Southend. He was Prince Arthur. He stayed in the Royal and was so delighted with his suite that he presented the landlord with his photograph—to beautify the room, presumably.

The Prince Imperial of France stayed here too, in 1874. In the October of that year he hunted the hare with beagles with Mr. E. Jackson, a well-known local sportsman.

The other Southend coaching house was the Ship. Wright's gazetteer stated: "The Ship hotel, which besides every necessary accommodation for comfort and convenience is supplied with hot and cold baths."

The Ship is for ever associated with the Nore mutiny, for it was there that the sailors used to meet to discuss their grievances—and grievances there were in plenty.

Another meeting in the Ship played an important part in the development of Southend. The date was March 30, 1829, and the subject for discussion was the proposed pier. When the matter was first suggested the previous year it met with considerable opposition, particularly from the fishermen, who feared that their livelihood would be affected. This meeting was convened by the directors to convince the opposition that their fears were groundless. They succeeded.

Whatever one thinks of Southend as a holiday resort, no one will deny that the walk along the front to Leigh—when the tide is in!—is as delightful as it is exhilarating. And what a different world the walker finds himself in on arriving in Leigh! It is still a fishing village in spite of its proximity to Southend, and it still possesses a period charm.

Behind this charm, however, there is a hard core of history, mostly of the nautical kind, of course. Among the scores of sailors produced by Leigh many rose to high rank in the Navy, but many more scorned the dignity of a uniform to indulge in various forms of private enterprise, particularly smuggling. Not that smuggling was a sinecure. The forces of the law were strong in this area, but this hazard added to the thrill of the run. As in the other areas of Essex we have visited, systems of signalling were practised and places of concealment were used. An obvious vantage point was Hadleigh Castle, easily seen from both the Kentish shore and

Fobbing church tower. Cock-lofts are numerous in the old village, and many a rear exit allowed for a quick escape to Daw's Heath behind.

The former Peter Boat was burnt down in 1892 after about 200 years of service. In the ruins a large underground chamber was discovered with access to the waterfront, and evidence of its use by smugglers was also observed.

As is the custom in many villages today, local societies used the inn as a meeting place. In the old Peter Boat assembled the Leigh Comicals, a fishermen's benevolent society founded about 1850. They derived their name from their official regalia. Their annual feast was on the first Wednesday in July, and it was cheaper to attend, and more enjoyable, than to be absent, since, although the dinner cost 3/6, absentees were fined 5/-.

The entertainment was on a lavish scale, and it is doubtful if the use of the society's funds was quite in accord with the constitution. Not that this thought troubled the participants—members, wives or sweethearts and guests—as they danced to a London band after enjoying the sumptuous banquet. But the scale of the entertainment told on the funds. Subscriptions had to be raised—an action which resulted in the resignation of a number of members.

The first of these benevolent societies was formed about 1830 and derived its name from the King's Head, where it held its meetings.

The United Brethren, popularly known as the " Billet Club " after the inn of the same name, was another society formed in 1853. Although the rules stated that only fishermen living within a mile of the Crooked Billet were eligible for membership, the local policeman was admitted, but he, unfortunately for the club, fell ill and received sickness benefit for such a long time that the club became " financially embarrassed."

Not only benevolent societies met in the local inns. Easter meetings of the vestry were also held, the cost in these cases being met from parish funds. In 1783, when the meeting was held in the Watermen's Arms, the cost was £1/14/9. Two years later the vestry met in the Queen's Head and the expenses were:

" For line (loin) of Veal to Easter Dinner	..		10s.	0
Beef for the Easter Meeting	..	..	..	11s.	8
Easter Meeting at Queen's Head		..	..	£1. 8s.	3 "

The cost of the meeting was more reasonable than that quoted for Barling, but tasty nevertheless.

The advent of the railway in 1854 was not a popular event, and the conservative fisherfolk did not look with favour on the navvies who worked on the construction. Fights after closing time were not uncommon. One incident is well remembered. A huge navvy known as " Fisty " led his gang to the Leigh public-houses and drank large quantities of the limited beer supplies. They had done this in the neighbouring villages, but nobody had felt strong enough to stop them. In Leigh, however, there was one man renowned for his fighting ability, " Snikey " Cotgrove, and he decided to settle the question " outside." As in all good stories, our hero thrashed the villain and the beer was saved for the villagers.

Following the coastline, we sail up the creek to South Benfleet. It is a fascinating region, colourful and steeped in ancient legend. Was it not here that Alfred defeated the Danes who in 893 had built a base camp from which they could raid and plunder the Saxon villages? So the *Anglo-Saxon Chronicle* records. Excavations seem to support the tale, for many human bones have been found among stakes charred by fire. The Anchor stands on part of the Danish earthworks. It was in this inn that the Bishop of Essex was said to have dined after consecrating the old church on Canvey Island in 1600. Old, too, is the Hoy and Helmet standing at the foot of the hill. It was built about 500 years ago when some unknown artist-craftsmen were creating the exquisite porch of the church on the hill behind. Neither the Anchor nor the Hoy and Helmet has led a blameless life. Who could in such a long existence? The crime committed beneath their roofs is one with which we are now familiar—smuggling. Inns occupying such positions were ideally situated for the illegal trade—a creek within 100 yards or so of their doorways, and high land behind for signalling and for keeping a lookout. Some ten years ago, when some structural alterations were being made to the Hoy and Helmet an unexpected chamber was found beneath the inn. A passage led from it to the church—so it is said.

One of the most interesting things about this inn is its unusual name. The simple explanation that the sign is in all probability an impaled one is not generally accepted. A more fanciful interpretation is given, linking the village with its exciting past. The

Hoy, it is claimed, is a Danish boat and the Helmet a primitive jetty constructed of packed earth and flints. This explanation has at least the merit of romance.

A solitary bridge connects the mainland to Canvey Island, on which, it has been said, the only building of interest is the Lobster Smack. The verdict is not far wrong—but one must not forget the two Dutch houses. The weatherboarded inn dates from 1563. The realization of all the history that has glided by on the neighbouring river since that date leaves one spellbound. Sailors of many nations, their ships lying quietly at anchor in Hole Haven, have sung of home while drinking in the low-ceilinged bar of the Lobster Smack. Dutchmen, feeling solidly prosperous on earnings derived from reclaiming the island, have shaken the beams with their guttural songs. And the number of amateur yachtsmen who have leaned on the bar can only have been equalled by the hordes of cockney trippers who sink their wallop with enormous gusto during the summer months.

Needless to say, the inn is not unconnected with smugglers. Indeed, if it had existed for its 400 years with an unsullied record it could be regarded as a curiosity. It was ideally situated for receiving contraband, and until comparatively recently Canvey was a lonely, wind-swept island.

There is one amusing smuggling story still repeated in the bars of the Lobster Smack. An island farmer implored the priest to visit his house with his whole congregation to exorcize the evil spirits that made life unbearable for him and his family. The priest readily agreed and spared no effort in helping his tormented parishioner. The latter, however, was not present at the ceremony. He was in church! Not from any religious motives, we must add, but in order to direct his fellow smugglers in the removal of the contraband which they had hidden there.

The Lobster Smack was sometimes used as changing quarters in the days of the knuckle fighters. The loneliness of the low marsh-lands made them an ideal spot for those fierce battles. Even now there are corners of the flats where the only sounds are the call of the sea-bird and the swish-swash of the water against the dykes. Standing in these quiet spots it is easy to imagine the clandestine gatherings of the spectators. No word had been published in the press that a fight was to take place, but shortly before the event the news spread from inn to inn along the Thames and the enthusiasts braved the uncomfortable journey to the Canvey marshes and evaded the vigilance of the police in order to support their favourite.

The most notable fight which took place on the island was probably that between Tom Sayers and Aaron Jones in January 1857. For sixty-five rounds these giants battered at each other. One hour, two hours—and still they were on their feet. Darkness gathered, and due to the failing light the referee had to stop the fight and declare a draw.

Across Hole Haven Creek, near Shell Haven, another fight took place five years later between " on my right, Jem Mace; and on my left, Tom King." This was a memorable encounter, since it was the last heavyweight championship to be fought in England without gloves. The fight was a comparatively short affair of twenty-one rounds and was won by King. He collected a belt and a purse of £300 for his historic victory.

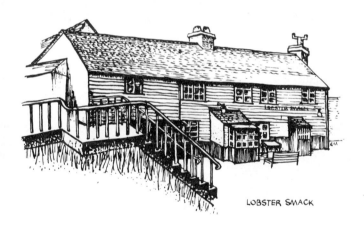

LOBSTER SMACK

CHAPTER XIII

REVOLTING INCIDENTS

THOSE old-time fighters and their supporters chose the Essex marshes for their rendezvous because of their remoteness and loneliness. How amazed they would be if they could see the same marshes today! They would scarcely recognize their venue amid the tremendous oil installations, but the inns of the neighbouring villages of Corringham and Fobbing would not seem unfamiliar.

The old Ship in Fobbing has been converted into houses. The building stands alongside Fobbing's minute harbour, from which the trade has long since departed. No longer do you hear the shouting and the curses of the bargemen loading the bricks made on the adjacent brickfield. Brick-making was thirsty work, but work which made one thirsty was a pleasure when an inn was so convenient!

Dickens knew the Thames-side flats well, and his fine descriptions are still true of much of this low-lying land. Some Dickensians even claim to have identified the Fobbing Ship as the one seen by Pip and his friends when they were helping the convict Magwitch to escape. The lighthouse described in *Great Expectations*—"a little, squat, shoal lighthouse on open piles, crippled on the mud on stilts and crutches"—sounds for all the world like Mucking lighthouse.

Climb the hill from the former Ship and you arrive at the church. Across the road from it stands the White Lion, an inn built largely in the fifteenth century. It still retains its stable yards and loose boxes—and the "regulars" still retain their memories of battles long ago. Scarcely is your pint drawn before a friendly stranger will mention the magic name of Jack Straw, as if he lived but yesterday. Jack, you will be told, was born and bred in Fobbing and it was he who led the local peasants on to London, only to be halted at Mile End by the young King Richard II, who persuaded them, with false promises, to return home. The cruel slaughter that belied those promises still tastes bitter in the mouths of those Fobbing " regulars." Drink again and deep, to wash away the taste of that betrayal.

Was the White Lion an inn in 1639? We do not know, but we do know that William Kie de eadem was drunk in that year, for his appearance before the magistrates is recorded. " He stated that by reason of an ague which he hath a long time, he was advised to make himselfe droncke and haply might forget himselfe in soe doing."

William's excuse was not accepted. He was made to apologize before the minister and guardians and pay a fine of 3/8.

That unique craft the Thames sailing barge is gradually becoming a museum piece, and even the inns connected with its heyday are being superseded by fashionable, plush roadhouses. So it is good to see one of the old inns once patronized by bargemen still carrying on a lively trade even though the clientele has changed. It was not so long ago that the White Lion's links with the river were more obvious than they are today. The stables at the rear were full of barge-gear—pulleys, buoys, anchors and ships' stores. In the bars villager and bargee swapped tales of their respective callings. But it was on Oak Apple Day, May 29, that the cares of their occupations were forgotten, for on that day, when the front of the White Lion was decorated with oak branches cut from neighbouring trees, the river men and villagers joined together in drinking and dancing into the late evening.

Readers of Defoe will perhaps recall that ague was a common complaint in these low-lying lands. He wrote that in this damp part of the world the men had a dozen and a half wives. The men " being bred in the marshes themselves and seasoned to the place, did pretty well with it, but that they always went up into the hilly country, or, to speak their own language, into the uplands for a wife, that when they took their lasses out of the wholesome and fresh air, they were healthy, fresh and clear, and well, but when they came out of their native air into the marshes among the fogs and damps, there they presently changed their complexion, got an ague or two, and seldom held it above half a year, or a year at the most. ' And then,' said he [his informant], ' we go into the uplands, to fetch another.' "

The White Lion stands at the junction of the Vange and Corringham roads, in which towns there are interesting inns. In Vange is the Five Bells. In 1769 it was known as the Six Bells, but some time in the intervening years it has suffered the fate of the wedding bell of the popular song. The inn is interesting and a shop and a smithy are attached to it.

In Corringham is the Bull inn. It has been suggested that the name is derived from the Boleyn or Bullen family, which is known to have held land in the neighbourhood. This is a good example of folk etymology. The sign is probably derived from the word " bulla "—a licence granted to certain inns to allow them to act as pilgrim rest houses. Apart from the suggestive name and the proximity of the church there is no direct evidence to support the claim, but the assumption is reasonable. That the number of pilgrims to Canterbury reached phenomenal figures is not questioned. They had to cross the Thames if they had travelled through Essex, and naturally made use of the numerous ferries. Can we doubt, therefore, that many sought shelter in the riverside inns? Why not in the Bull then?

The Bull is an ancient house. The cross-wing with overhanging gable is about 500 years old and most of the remainder of the building is only 200 years younger.

Stories of smuggling are rife in the neighbourhood and, needless to say, the Bull features in many of them—with very good reason, for some of the structural features of the house are unusual, to say the least. Double walls, sliding panels, secret cellars and concealed chambers in chimneys did not usually exist for honest purposes.

For centuries the life of the village revolved around the church and the inn, and the juxtaposition of these two buildings never seemed out of place. In Corringham the wide road between the inn and the church wall was used for the weekly market and for the annual fair. Against the wall itself stood the village stocks. Was the position of this instrument calculated to add to the punishment of the unhappy felon? While he sweltered in the summer heat, thirsty villagers assuaged themselves across the road. Perhaps they passed him a surreptitious tankard, but not, we think, when Abraham Bell was landlord, for he was parish constable too in the days of the third George.

Of the two old inns in the neighbouring town of Stanford-le-Hope, the King's Head and the Cock and Pie, only the former now remains and that much altered. At one time it was a stopping place for the Southend coach. The Cock and Pie stood next to Barclays Bank, overlooking the green and the church beyond. It was a one-storied building, constructed of weatherboard. When it started as an inn is impossible to say, but in the register of St. Margaret's church is the entry: " Thomas Tomlinson, a stranger, dyed at Ye Cock and Magpie and was buried 25th April 1701."

A sad tale links the two inns.

Just over 100 years ago two fishermen were plying their trade in Shell Haven Creek when Captain Moir, an ex-soldier who farmed land adjacent to the river, saw them and ordered them away. They refused. Having fished there for years they saw no reason why they should not continue the practice. Angrily the captain turned on his heel and strode away.

Some time later one of the fishermen landed with some fish, which he took to the nearby cottage of Mrs. Baker and exchanged for some potatoes. On returning to his boat he again met Captain Moir, who was now armed and accompanied by his groom. Since the captain objected to strangers fishing off his land it is hardly surprising that he should strongly resent anyone walking on it. Words flew, tempers rose, and to strengthen his argument the captain shot the fisherman, wounding him in the arm. Malcolm, for that was his name, collapsed, and was carried to the cottage by his mate and the bailiff. There he lay until a doctor arrived from Stanford and took him in his horse and trap to the Cock and Pie. He was put to bed, but, due to the loss of blood, died shortly afterwards.

The inquest was held in the King's Head and lasted six hours. Captain Moir was committed to the Essex Assizes.

The trial took place during the month of August 1830. In his defence the captain said that he always carried pistols in his pocket, as the area was so deserted and many outrages had been committed there.

No one denied the truth of this statement, but it was argued that it did not give him the right to shoot trespassers. He was found guilty of murder and ordered to be hanged, his body to be dissected after the execution.

Wharf Road leads from the Green, Stanford-le-Hope, to a path which wanders across the Warren, a region of abandoned gravel pits, to Mucking, a village prettier than its name. The former

Crown inn is now a dwelling house gaily bedecked, in season, with the loveliest flowers. Was it in the old Crown that John Smith, yeoman, and his friends Edward Drywood, husbandman, and John Bottle, miller, forgathered for their drinking bouts? We do not know, but we do know that their behaviour disturbed the customary peace of Mucking in the year 1621. The matter reached a head on August 10 of that year when the three friends went to church, and no sooner had John Coshe uttered the words " I would not admit to the Sacrament any of my parish which I knew to be common blasphemers or drunkards " than " up jumped Smith straightway—a common disturber of the King's peace— and announced in a loud voice, ' There is the end of the Text,' to the great disturbance of Coshe and the parishioners in the church."

THE BULL INN · CORRINGHAM

The HOY & HELMET
S·BENFLEET

HOT CROSS BUNS

"THE BELL"· HORNDON-ON-THE-HILL

THE BE[...]
HORNDO[...]
ON - THE - H[...]

THE CRANE · BASILDON

CHAPTER XIV

EAST TILBURY TO CHELMSFORD

AS we travel westwards we enter a part of Essex which has been much maligned, wrongly in my opinion. If the wanderer forsakes the main roads he will be delighted to find villages of quiet charm, and sometimes of great beauty. In almost all these villages are inns of interest. Few have a tale to tell, but to the connoisseur of inns this is not always necessary. Atmosphere and the company are enough. To sit in the forecourt of the Harrow, Bulphan, for instance, of a warm summer evening, when the only sounds are made by the friendly farm animals and the poultry grubbing in the yard, is pure delight, particularly if one has just escaped from the monstrous hordes of traffic returning Londonwards after a day in Southend.

Nowadays the main traffic in south Essex is east to west, but this has not always been the case. A glance at a map reveals the great number of roads running southwards to the river. On reflection, this is just what one would expect, for, generally speaking, to travel parallel to the Thames over this part of Essex is to journey against what might be called the historical grain of the county. Until the comparatively recent growth of Southend as a seaside resort and the consequent development of the arterial roads out of London to the south-eastern fringe of Essex, travellers from time immemorial have found it much easier to travel southwards towards the Thames than eastwards across the Essex lowlands. Soldier, merchant and pilgrim have followed these ancient paths. However, when one thinks of the Romans in this connection problems immediately arise. It is known, for instance, that on the riverside at East Tilbury there were a ferry terminal and an important entrepôt for pottery, but to date no road has been found to connect the site with any inland settlement, although it is fairly certain that one or more must have existed. As far as I know nobody has carried out any research on the subject. In the Middle Ages the pilgrim traffic south to Canterbury and north to Walsingham reached considerable proportions. To me this suggests a great number of ferries. Those at Tilbury, Grays, West Thurrock, Purfleet and Rainham are of ancient origin and were active until fairly recent times, but there must have been many others to cope with the great number of pilgrims. In one of the following chapters we shall follow the traditional pilgrim route from Brentwood to the West Thurrock ferry, but before we make that journey let us first travel from East Tilbury to Chelmsford, then from Tilbury Fort to Brentwood along routes as old as time.

East Tilbury is a small riverside village with memories of St. Cedd, the Dutch and General Gordon. The saint built a monastery, the Dutch bowled over the church tower and the general built the ugly fort. At the junction of the village high road with the road coming from West Tilbury stands the George and Dragon. From Cary's *New Itinerary* of 1828 we find that the route taken by the London coach to Southend passed the George and Dragon on its journey through Rainham, Wennington, Purfleet, West Thurrock, Grays Thurrock, Little Thurrock, Chadwell, West Tilbury, Mucking-ford, Mucking, Stanford, Vange and on to South End [*sic*].

Mucking's former inn we have already noticed. We continue north to Horndon-on-the-Hill, where the sign of the Bell greets us. The coachway and much of the building were built in the seventeenth century, but the most interesting part of the structure is on the north side—500-year-old post-and-pan timbering.

Inside the Bell, nailed to one of the old ceiling beams, are a number of round dark objects which, on closer inspection, turn out to be hot-cross buns in progressive stages of fossilization. This strange custom was begun in the year 1900 and is still maintained. In 1954 the Bell celebrated its 400th anniversary as a licensed house by hanging a garland of laurel on its sign—a happy revival of an ancient practice. Although not the only old inn in the village—the White Hart and the Swan are frequently mentioned in the manor rolls of Ardern Hall—it was the only coaching inn, a daily stage leaving for the Bull inn, Aldgate, via Orsett, North Stifford and Aveley. Some old milestones can still be seen along this route between Horndon and Stifford.

Was Thomas Higbed the martyr burned to death in the field behind the Bell? There is no actual record, but the strong tradition still persists. Higbed was a Horndon man of some wealth, but to him the world's goods were as nothing compared with the gifts of heaven. He was tried at the Consistory of St. Paul's on February 17, 1555, and when asked to recant and embrace Catholicism he said, according to Foxe: " I have been of this mind and opinion these sixteen years, and do what you can you shall do no more than God will permit, and with what measure ye mete to us, look for the same at God's hands."

For fourteen days he was imprisoned at Newgate, then taken by the Sheriff of Essex, William Harvard of Pitsea, first to Brentwood, where he and other condemned men were made to witness the burning of Hunter, then to Horndon-on-the-Hill, where he met his death on March 26, 1555.

Queen Elizabeth passed the Bell inn in the Armada year. She landed at Tilbury Fort and stayed that night in the house of Sir Thomas Rich in Horndon-on-the-Hill. Rich's place was known as Arderne Hall, but the present farm of the same name is not the original building, although the small building in the rear was probably seen by the great queen.

From the farm the land slopes, gradually at first, then steeply, to Langdon Hill, on the summit of which is an inn named the Crown, not because of its position but because it stands on land which belonged at one time to the Crown. Its sign, well modelled, stands in relief on the façade.

The view from the lookout on the inn roof is truly magnificent, but even from ground level the extensive panorama is quite impressive, although perhaps not quite as wonderful as Arthur Young's description in his *Southern Tour*: " One of the most astonishing prospects to be beheld breaks out almost at once upon one of the dark lanes. Such a prodigious valley, everywhere painted with the finest verdure, and intersected with numerous hedges and woods, appears beneath you that it is past description; the Thames winding through it, full of ships and bounded by the hills of Kent. Nothing can exceed it, except that which Hannibal exhibited to his disconsolate troops, when he bade them behold the glories of the Italian plains."

If Young could return now and see the sprawl that is Laindon, how he would rant! The town has nothing to detain us and it is with relief that we escape again to the countryside beyond and to the ancient delights of Billericay.

Before we reach the town, however, it is well worth while following the Little Burstead road for a short distance to see what modern décor has done to the Duke's Head. Do not be misled by the red-brick exterior so reminiscent of late-Victorian station waiting rooms. One step beyond the threshold and—*Ole!*—you are in a Spanish hacienda, or at least the Essex version of one. Archways have taken the place of doorways, and some ironwork grill *à l'espagnol* in an alcove and the gay wallpaper in all the rooms smacks of the Costa Brava! It comes as a shock when drinking in such exotic surroundings to look through the window and see not fountains gurgling beneath palm trees but an unkempt common scattered with gorse bushes and clumps of trees. One wonders if the décor was inspired by the campaigns of the duke whose head bedecks the inn.

On to Billericay, with its fascinating High Street, where the buildings of every age from medieval times to the present day are a feast for the antiquarian. But our interests are limited, though not without historic interest. The Sun shines on us at the crossroads. It is not more than two centuries old. At one time another inn called the Half Moon stood opposite, and the little cottage standing in between was known, not unnaturally, as the " Eclipse."

On the right along the High Street is another inn of about the same age as the Sun—the White Hart. A Parliament clock inside the house is believed to have been made by Daniel Cornell, who lived there at one time. Hay-carters used the inn a great deal, and a twice-weekly carrier service operated between here and Brentwood in the 1860s.

The field behind the inn is now built upon, but formerly many a keen cricket match was played there.

In 1776, for example, the *Chelmsford and Colchester Chronicle* contained the following announcement: " To be played at the White Hart at Billericay on 15th June, 1776. A Match of Cricket between 11 picked Gentlemen of Barstable and Chafford Hundreds against 11 of Billericay for 11 Gold Laced Hats. The wickets will be pitched at 10 o'clock and the Match played out."

Across the road is the Red Lion, a building which is not only one of the oldest in the old village, but has a licence dating back to 1593! So Christopher and Marie Martin, Solomon Prower and John Langerman must have passed it when, in 1620, they walked down the hill for the last time on their way to Leigh, the *Mayflower* and the New World.

For 400 years, then, the Red Lion has run like a thread through the town's history, and there is little doubt that this thread will be extended several more centuries. In the past the court leet and baron was held here, presided over by the lords of the manor— the Petre family. At these meetings, which took place in the first part of Whitsun week, the affairs of Billericay were settled for the following year—" the appointment of the Constable, Ale-Taster and other officials, and Admittance of the new tenants or Surrender of the old ones to the Copyhold Property together with other legal matters and even the regulation of the Market."

These tasks completed, no doubt everyone felt relieved, and spent the rest of the week celebrating in the time-honoured manner.

In 1848 the licensee was Richard Mumford, who made " a bit on the side " by acting as agent for the London Corporation Fire and Life Assurance Company. This same Richard could also supply " Post-Horses, close and open Carriages, Flys, Gigs, etc." An enterprising man.

The Red Lion was still a posting house in 1874 as well as the Inland Revenue office.

To celebrate the Diamond Jubilee an ox was roasted and served to the villagers on tables which had been erected on the roadway outside the inn.

A little farther along the High Street is a fingerpost pointing to an old coachway. It does not proclaim this fact today, but supports the legends " Public conveniences " and " Ministry of Food." Along the alleyway are stables which, with some cellars beneath the neighbouring houses and Grenville House, are the only remains of the old Crown. Its licence was as old as that of the Red Lion, and in the coaching era its business was even more important. The original buildings consisted of the inn proper in the High Street, the Crown tap in Chapel Street, and the brewery standing between.

In 1823 the Tilbury coach called at the Bell, Horndon-on-the-Hill, and the Crown, Billericay, and from Cary's *Great Roads* of 1828 we learn that the coaches from the Bull, Aldgate, also stopped at the Crown before proceeding via Rayleigh, Hadleigh, Leigh, Rochford and Prittlewell to South End.

Twenty-five years later the Southend coach left the King's Head, Rochford, three times a week and passed through Rayleigh and Billericay. The landlord at this time was a horse and gig owner,

and a wine and spirit merchant as well as a brewer, and the license
of the Crown tap was a blacksmith.

The Crown did not survive the coming of the railway, although
the brewery still carried on for a time. The name, however, did no
die out. In 1862 it was adopted by an inn in the High Street and i
1890 it moved to its present position opposite the Railway Hotel.

Near the junction of the High Street with Chapel Street stand
the Chequers, built about 400 years ago. Much of the original
structure still remains, but alterations and additions have, of cours
taken place. There are some grounds for believing that before
became an inn it was a chantry farmhouse. Behind it still stands-
but only just!—the chantry barn. Its walls are constructed in th
same manner as the nave of Greensted church, that is of spl
tree trunks. In the nettles which grow in abundance near th
building is an old bellows. It belonged to the Pease brothers, wh
used the building as their depot, for they were carriers to Southen
and London.

The first chapter of this book dealt briefly with the Welsh drover
Most of them, after visiting Essex, returned to the land of the
fathers, but some, like the Spittys of Hurlocks, stayed on an
became property owners. The name Spitty seems to be derive
from Yspytty Ystwyth, a town in Cardiganshire.

Beyond Billericay the road meanders through pleasant country
climbing gradually all the time to Stock and beyond.

Almost the first building to be seen inside Stock parish boundar
is a large modern inn called, rather misleadingly, the Old King
Head—an old head on a young body. The actual village is a shor
way beyond, and in order to continue northwards one has to swin
around the Cock, which stands foursquare across one's path
Quite near but off the main road is a smaller but older inn, th
Bear. Its attractive front is matched by a most interesting an
varied rear. Nor is the inside disappointing. The snug lounge i
embellished with horse brasses, stirrups, post-horns, huntin
horns, whips, switches and a framed photograph of a M.O.F
In such an atmosphere one is not surprised to hear much talk c
hunting, horses and country matters in general. The visitor wi
not have downed his first drink before hearing about Old Spide.
He was an ostler who spent his spare time drinking in the Bea
He also had a strange habit when in his cups of crawling up th
chimney in one bar and down the chimney in the next. Sometime

he varied the procedure by not descending until the following day. Nobody seemed surprised. They assumed that Old Spider had found a forgotten bacon loft in which he could sleep off the effects of the drink.

His movements were quiet and unobtrusive and he came and went without comment from the regulars. When he ceased to appear some did wonder where he had gone—but it was not until twenty years later that they found out! During renovations the smoked body of the old ostler was found stuck between the chimneys!

A mile or two outside Stock is a rambling building which has been converted into an inn and called the Ship. The view from the outside is extensive, being uninterrupted by any building for miles.

Between the Ship and the town of Chelmsford lies Galleywood Common. It was in the summer time that I went there, and the silhouette of the common against a sky of dreamy white clouds was memorable. The eye followed the chervil-lined road winding between cornfields to the very tall steeple soaring above a rich variety of green foliage. Lovely it was that day, but I am told that the best time to visit the common is when the thousands of gorse bushes are a blaze of gold.

A race-track encircles the common, but nobody seems to know when horse racing started here, although it is known that steeple-chasing replaced the flat racing that had been popular since the middle of the eighteenth century. Those were the days! Horse racing was not the only attraction—cock-fighting went on near the site of the present pavilion, prizefighting attracted excited crowds, and in front of the Admiral Rous—now a tea garden to the south of the grandstand—dancing of a rather hectic variety was enjoyed. The inn itself was used as a sort of unofficial grand-stand, for it was not until 1863 that the present one was built.

CHAPTER XV

TILBURY FORT TO BRENTWOOD

THERE is nothing old in Tilbury town for the simple reason that until the coming of the railway less than a century ago the only building on the site was a solitary structure standing in the centre of the marshes. It was not even an inn—in fact it was quite the opposite, for a map of 1801 labels it "milkhouse."

Although the town is modern the celebrated fort is, of course, a scheduled "ancient monument," and the old road from the north met the river at this point. From here ran the former ferry to Kent, and it was very natural, therefore, that an inn should spring up to provide sustenance for the hungry and thirsty travellers. This inn was named the World's End—although the sign is not so appropriate nowadays since the growth of Tilbury town. Formerly it was called the Suttling House, that is a house where troops were provisioned. One "caretaker" of the fort, no doubt well acquainted with the military thirst, combined his routine job with that of landlord of the inn, and again in 1631 the Commissioner for Ordnance reported: "No man lodgeth within the Fort but the Master-Gunner, who keepeth a victualling house for fisherfolks near adjoining, a disparagement of His Majesty's Service."

Outside the World's End the old mounting block still remains. Looking riverwards, one sees above the dyke barge sails and the funnels of great liners moving silently and detached.

A ferry in the vicinity of this spot seems to have operated from time immemorial. In 1798 it was proposed to connect the two banks of the Thames by tunnel. To advance this project a public meeting was held in Gravesend with Earl Darnley in the chair. A resolution was passed that a tunnel be built to connect Gravesend with the Tilbury shore. Money was actually subscribed, but, like many a beautiful bubble, the good resolution burst.

IND COOPE

THE CHEQUERS

E CHEQUERS
ILLERICAY

GM.

THE BOAR'S
· HERONGA

THE HARROW · BULPHAN

1963

Of the innumerable passengers who used the old ferry one of the immortals was Nick Nevinson, or "Swift Nicks" as he was called. It was he and not Dick Turpin who performed the astonishing feat of riding from Rochester to York in about twelve hours!

Late one night Nevinson held up a coach on Gad's Hill, and believing that one of the occupants had recognized him he headed immediately for the Gravesend ferry, which he crossed at about four o'clock in the morning and then rode hard all day to reach York that same evening. There he made himself known to the mayor, who was playing bowls, a gambit which stood him in good stead later when he was accused of the hold-up. Since no one would believe that anyone could perform such a fantastic ride "Swift Nicks" was acquitted.

The first leg of Nicks's Essex route would have taken him to West Tilbury, a sleepy village blissfully unaware of its tremendous connections with history. Romans, St. Cedd, Normans, Gervaise de Tillebery, Queen Elizabeth I, General Fairfax—all are connected with it. And in the days of the stage-coach how many more of the great ones of the country stepped into the King's Head to partake of ale or the famed Tilbury water we can but imagine. At West Tilbury passengers desirous of proceeding to Kent transferred to the ferry coach. In those days the little village was a busy place and all available accommodation was frequently taken, particularly during wartime. Indeed, it was to cope with this influx that the Bell was built in 1780. About a century later, when travel by coach was almost a thing of the past and West Tilbury was slipping back into its former role of a small country village, the Rev. Sir Adam Gordon, Bart., bought the Bell for £700 and presented it to the parish to serve as a vicarage.

We have already followed the road to Billericay, a road which gave Arthur Young no pleasure when he travelled over it in 1771: "Of all the cursed roads that ever disgraced this Kingdom, none ever equalled that from Billericay to the King's Head at Tilbury."

Our present route takes us to Chadwell St. Mary, where the Cross Keys stands, not inappropriately, opposite the church, and on to Orsett Cock. The present building is modern, but occupies the site of a former inn of the same name. Crossing the Grays—Southend road we soon arrive at Orsett village, where the Whitmore

Arms displays the shield of arms of Col. Sir Francis Whitmore,
Lord-Lieutenant of Essex, whose mansion, so well known to the
Royal Family, stands nearby.

It is worth while deserting our direct route for a moment in
order to visit the King's Arms in Baker Street. A rustic pub in the
heart of the West End would strike an odd note. Here in an Essex
hamlet we find a village inn with a West End décor!

We return to Orsett and continue northwards, but again a
diversion to the Harrow, Bulphan, is not without interest, since
one can obtain a good idea of what a medieval alehouse looked
like—and this is said with no disrespect. In those far-off days a
bar—the all-important feature of today's public-houses—was
non-existent. The thirsty man entered the kitchen of mine host
and sat down to his refreshment among the family. The Harrow
has not quite this intimacy, but one still feels that one is in a private
house. There is no bar, the drinks being served through a small
hatch. Outside too there is the same homely touch. This is no
super-arterial-road pull-in, but the domestic yard. There is no
pretence. One sits in a farmyard. Chickens strut and peck for
whatever they do peck for, horses crane their necks over the gate
for a pat or a titbit, and on the roof of the barn a house-leek has
created a live and intricate mosaic.

There is no inn in Bulphan proper—if any part of this very scattered village can make that claim. The group of houses on the
Brentwood road is certainly one centre. Appleton's Farm, now
a café, was at one time the Plough inn with a tradition that Henry
VIII sometimes " popped in for a quick one " (as a villager informed me) while on his way to see his lady love in Jericho. How
he got to Bulphan is not explained. Surprisingly, the same villager
did not claim that Queen Elizabeth had slept there in spite of the
fact that the building was standing in her day.

At the intersection of the Brentwood road with the Southend
arterial road stands a large inn known as Halfway House, which
marks half the thirsty journey from London to Southend. During
the summer season stalls are set up on the large pull-in for displaying
the winkles, cockles, jellied eels and other sea-food dear to the
palates of London's East Enders, and accordions provide the
accompaniment to sprightly renderings of " Knees up Mother
Brown," the " Lambeth Walk," and the cockney anthem, " London
Town." Such a good time is spent at the Halfway House that one

wonders why anyone proceeds to Southend. Some do not—they meet the coach coming back!

It might interest television addicts that one episode of the programme series called " Z Cars " was shot at the Halfway House.

This road to Southend is, of course, of quite recent origin. The former east—west roads meandered pleasantly from village to village. The inns that served the traveller were simple village inns with no pretensions to luxury, but each had its individual characteristics. Now the inns or roadhouses that have sprung up at intervals along the arterial road are all, more or less, cast in the same mould: enormous pull-ins for cars and coaches; lounge bars lined with oak panelling and furnished with carpets, glass or formica-topped tables and comfortable arm-chairs. There is scarcely any difference between these modern inns whether they be in Essex or Cornwall, and even the clientele is of a pattern!

We leave the Southend atmosphere of the Halfway House forecourt and, within half a mile, are once again deep in the Essex countryside. A pictorial village sign informs us that we are in Herongate. The main road sweeps through, but the older side road leads to the Green Man, also identifiable by a pictorial sign, this time of Robin Hood. The Green Man is pleasant enough at any time, but never more so than after a cricket match. Herongate is fortunate to possess a charming village green, and what a delightful experience it is to sit in the shade of the giant trees, lazily watching a local match, and when the game is over to stroll to the Green Man and discuss the day's play over a long drink of cool ale—surely one of England's contributions to the proper enjoyment of leisure.

The Boar's Head, too, is the kind of inn that one associates with village cricket. It stands where a side road strikes off the Brentwood road for Billericay. It is a mellow inn and its inside is as warm and cosy as its red roof suggests. Old settles, horse-brasses and coaching horns add an authentic touch of age, but one of its more attractive features is the series of bay windows along one of its walls, affording a view of the pond and the pleasant garden.

A short distance along the road to Billericay is the Old Dog, a picturesque weatherboarded inn which enjoys a surprising popularity. Perhaps the unusually low ceilings and the feeling of warmth and friendliness arising out of the forced intimacy of the minute rooms contribute. It has been said that because the rooms are so small you have to be careful not to pour your drink down your neighbour's throat!

Beyond Herongate the Ingrave Road skirts the woods surrounding Thorndon Hall before entering Brentwood—and before entering Brentwood you should most certainly wander through the woods. Many roads and paths lead on to Warley Common, a high ground fringed by trees and commanding an extensive view to the Thames and beyond. The one drawback is its considerable popularity, but there is always the Greyhound, a most pleasant retreat at any time.

The OLD DOG
HERONGATE

CHAPTER XVI

IN THE PATH OF THE PILGRIMS

THE abbot of St. Osyth built a chapel in Brentwood and dedicated it to St. Thomas the Martyr. The ruins can still be seen in the High Street. Morant adds some interesting details: " The Chaplain . . . was to swear that he would not knowingly injure the mother church [of South Weald]; that he would not receive any parishioners to divine offices, Communion, Confessions, or Purifications, on Sundays or holidays, without the Parson's express leave; except on the day of St. Thomas's Passion or Translation and the time of the fair. Nor shall there be any Baptism or Burial of the dead. . . . The offerings that are made by strangers and passengers shall be entirely for the maintenance of the Chaplain. . . . The perquisites of this Chaplain arose from travellers upon the road, and such as came out of devotion to Saint Thomas; whence a gate upon the way from Ongar in this parish retains the name of Pilgrim's Hatch . . ."

By which route did the pilgrims travel to reach the Thames? No one can say with certainty, but it is safe to assume that there was more than one way southwards. Some historians will not accept any of the roads that lead out of Brentwood because there is no factual evidence. In my opinion this is carrying the historical method too far. The road passing through the Ockendons to West Thurrock has been accepted by countless generations of Thurrockians as a pilgrim route, and it is up to the historians to prove that it was not so.

After all, there is some circumstantial evidence to support the claim. From a number of points along the route the Thames or Kent could be seen by the pilgrims; it was the most direct route from Brentwood to the river, and the villages were fairly close together, a fact of some importance in the Middle Ages, when travelling could be dangerous.

Where did these passengers and pilgrims stay overnight? The answer has already been given—in the hostels provided by the religious bodies. With the increase of traffic in the Middle Ages this accommodation proved inadequate, so inns were built which gradually supplanted the religious establishments. Some of the older inns of Brentwood which we have already visited were, no doubt, built with this specific intention.

From the chapel of St. Thomas we turn our steps southwards, following more or less the way of the medieval pilgrim. In Great Warley, the Headley Arms arrests our attention because of its delightful position. It stands on the far side of a pond decorated with ducks, and is backed by the pleasant woods of Warley Gap. On one side of the inn is a charming tea-garden, on the other a riding school.

Up to the middle of last century the Headley Arms was known by the more rural name of Magpie, and this is the sign which appears regularly in the annual register of alehouses between 1769 and 1828. The change draws attention to the Winne family, who purchased the manor of Great Warley in 1669. Sir George Winne, a baron of the Court of Exchequer in Scotland, was raised to the peerage in 1797 and took the title of Lord Headley, Baron Allanson and Winne of Aghadoe, County Kerry. The manor remained in the hands of the same family until the 1930s.

Dick Turpin is supposed to have been active in this neighbourhood, and naturally a hide-out must be devoted to the legend! It is to be found upstairs in the Headley Arms—a low-ceilinged room containing a cupboard which conceals an escape route to the woods. An adjoining bedroom is named after the cut-throat.

A mile or so down the road is another inn, equally picturesque, called the Thatchers. Two lovely trees grace the front courtyard, their foliage forming a pleasant canopy in the summer time for those who like taking to drink in the continental manner. Inside, arranged along the shelves in glass cases, are numerous dolls bedecked in national costumes.

Two ways south are open to us: the more direct across the arterial road to St. Mary's Lane and Clay Tye Hill to the Ockendons or the slightly more tortuous one through the lovely woods to Upminster Common, then south again via Hall Lane to Upminster. The second is perhaps preferable, not only for its beauty but also because it leads us to the town and the Bell. This inn was built by

Sir James Esdaile about the year 1765 when he became lord of the manor of Gaynes, but a hostel had existed on the site long before that date.

When the original Bell was built we do not know, but the Water Poet mentions it in 1636 when the landlady was Elizabeth Saward. References in parish records seem to indicate that an inn existed near the church before that date, but since no name is given we cannot be sure.

In 1761 the landlord was Isaac Bone, and like many another publican of those days he had other interests. His was carpentering, for his name appears frequently in the overseers' accounts in connection with the making of coffins or the village stocks.

The position of the building erected in 1765 has had an important influence upon the development of Upminster, although this is no place to discuss this story. When it was built it was the centre of a small village built around the green. A pond occupied the site of the car park—a pond which, on occasions, was to prove a dangerous hazard.

" On Tuesday the 11th instant the servants of a gentleman near the Bell, Upminster, having cleaned a smokejack, went into a pond to wash themselves, when one of them, Thomas Perry, who could not swim, went out of his depth, but was taken out in less than a minute to all appearance dead, but by making use of the proper methods, bleeding, etc., he so far recovered as to say he should not die then, and seemed cheerful, but on their going to give him a vomit he sank down and expired instantly." This is from the *Chelmsford Chronicle* of June 21, 1765. The pond lingered on, according to the local historian, Wilson, until 1850, when it was filled in and made into the Bell garden.

Mention of village prizefights taking place on the lonely Essex marshes has already been made. Sometimes the fights took place on equally isolated spots away from the river. The followers were frequently a disreputable crowd and indulged boisterously in near-orgies in the inn nearest the contests. When James Purkis was landlord (1824-31) he was terrified into inaction by the drunken invasion of the supporters of the champion pugilist, Josh Hudson.

They helped themselves to the drink. The local rector, who was also a magistrate, decided that discretion was the better part of valour and sent for the squire, Champion Edward Branfill, of Upminster Hall. Mounted on his old Waterloo charger Jumbo, the squire fearlessly rode through the crowd to the open carriage in which Hudson was sitting and forbade him to fight in Essex. " Sir " replied the champ, " from the very courteous and gentlemanly way you have addressed us I give you my word it shall not come off in this county." Wilson adds: " His promise was faithfully kept. The company proceeded to a part of Kent north of the Thames, where the fight was duly carried out."

Wilson sometimes dabbled in verse. The following he penned in 1896 as a compliment to Mrs. Henry Day, wife of the landlord, after she had been at the Bell for forty years:

> Compliments hearty on forty years stay—
> The time you'll complete by the close of the day.
> May your health remain good and your comforts be many,
> And the days yet to come be the happiest of any.
> I'll call in the morning, and tho' not stay to dine,
> We'll drink to your health in a glass of your wine;
> Then peacefully leave without more ado,
> And remain your well-wisher, T.L.W.

We are indebted to Wilson for his researches into Upminster history.

Mrs. Day retired eight years later, in 1904, and died in 1907 in Locksley Villa across the road from the Bell.

The landlord of the Bell pulled his last drink on Sunday, October 23, 1962. The merciless march of the affluent society bulldozes every obstacle from its path. If a building, however historic, however beautiful, interferes with the free flow of traffic, that building must be demolished. No one would claim that the Bell was of the highest order æsthetically, but architecturally it was one of the interesting buildings of Upminster and a link with the past. But it was in the way! So in December 1962 it was pulled down. There remains an emptiness in the heart of Upminster—and memories.

The main interest for us in Hornchurch is not the inns but the church, for inside this prominent and attractive building are two ringers' jugs—exactly half the number still to be found in Essex. The larger is a magnificent specimen, twenty inches high and fifty inches round its widest part. It is not perfectly symmetrical, but this in no way detracts. Its robustness and lack of any subtle refinement is in the tradition of English medieval pottery. Standing as it does on the north side of the church, the jug is not well placed to reveal the rich purply depths of its thick glaze. The inscription engraved on the clay body records the date, May 24, 1815; states that Rt. Aungier was the maker; and lists the names of the ringers. It is known that the jug was made in the local pottery of C. Cove which used to be situated at the western side of the High Street.

The smaller pitcher is older and, although more carefully made, lacks the virility of its neighbour. The glaze, too, is lacking in depth and brilliance. It is thirteen and a half inches high and forty inches in girth. An inscription in a cursive hand records the fact that it was made in 1731 in Hornchurch, Essex, and a list of the churchwardens is also given.

It is obvious from the inscriptions that the pitchers were specially made for use in the church, but somehow or other they found their way to that old coaching inn at the foot of church hill the King's Head. How long they were there we do not know, but we learn of their existence when they were seized in distraint for rent by the owners of the Hornchurch brewery, Henry and Benjamin Holmes. When Colonel and Mrs. Holmes died an auction was held in their home, the Towers, and members of the family purchased the jugs and presented them to the church on condition that they remained there permanently. Nowadays they stand innocently enough on the window sills, but their proper place is in the ringing chamber. *The Church Bells of Essex* records a set of rules that was formerly displayed in that chamber:

> " If you ring with Spur or Hat,
> Three pints of beer you pay for that;
> If you swear or give the Lye,
> A pot you pay Immediatly;
> If a bell you overthrow,
> A pint you pay before you go.   T.T.S. 1798 "

Those were the days! Beer was a much more popular thirst quencher than tea in those days, for did not the vestry frequently adjourn to the King's Head rather than to a " cosy café "? And most probably the beer mentioned in the following extract from the overseers' account was obtained in the vestry's favourite inn.

	s.	d.
For a coffin for a broom man yt dyed in ye Cage ..	8.	0
For an olde blankett for ye same man	2.	0
For beer for ye men yt carried him to buriall ..	3.	0
For stripping ye same man	1.	0

The White Hart is quite near the King's Head. The present building is large and modern, built to replace the original which was burnt down on November 7, 1872, the original being regarded by many as the most picturesque building in the old village. On its main chimney-stack was a large sundial. Today's inn has a large sign of a baying hart standing over the front entrance.

Does the White Hart stand on the site of a monastery? In 1158 some envoys of Henry II encountered difficulties while crossing the Alps, but were rescued by the monks of the famous hospice of St. Bernard. In gratitude the order was allowed by the king to set up a religious house in Havering and moneys for its upkeep were obtained from a royal grant of land. The tradition that Hornchurch had a monastery arises from the fact that a prior and twelve monks did move into the district, but information is too slight to form any conclusion as to their subsequent actions.

At one time Hornchurch was famed in Essex for its high standard of cricket, so it is not surprising that the town has a Cricketers' Arms. The club was founded in 1782 and at one time was undefeated for a period of seven years. But the feats of which it was most proud were its defeat of an all-Essex team and the drawn game with the M.C.C. on June 10, 1831.

Visiting teams were entertained alternately at the White Hart and the Bull. In 1825, for instance, after a return match with Fobbing—which the home team won—" the gentlemen then retired to the Bull inn, where after partaking of a most excellent dinner, provided by Mr. Gooch, the landlord, they were amused by some excellent songs, and the evening passed off with the greatest conviviality." Over the entrance to the inn's car park is the sign " Bull in "!

Hornchurch was noted too for sports other than cricket. North of the church, in a part of the Millfield known as the Dell, cockfights and prizefights took place. Charles Perfect, in his book *Ye Olde Village of Hornchurch*, quotes two newspaper cuttings for the year 1769 which indicate that the former were widely known and were patronized by men of rank:

" At Hornchurch in Essex last week Mr. Crump beat Lord Waltham by many bouts ahead; Champ Feeder for Mr. Crump and Dorrill of Chelmsford for Lord Waltham."

" The third annual Cock Match between the Gentlemen of London and the Gentlemen of Essex was fought at Hornchurch on Monday, Tuesday and Wednesday last. There were 36 bouts in the main, and 19 Byes, out of which the Essex Gentlemen won 36 bouts in the main and 11 byes."

Of the prizefights the most noteworthy took place on April 15, 1795, for a stake of 200 guineas a side between young Mendoza the Jew and the redoubtable John Jackson. The contest drew a crowd of over 3,000, including the Duke of Hamilton, Lord Delaval and Sir John Phillipson.

Betting started at 5 to 4 on Mendoza, but by the seventh round the odds had changed to 2 to 1 on Jackson. In the ninth and last round Jackson was supreme and a severely punished and utterly exhausted Mendoza acknowledged his defeat. His victor appeared quite fresh and unscathed.

The origins of the traditional wrestling bout that took place on Christmas Day are lost in antiquity. In the final years of the event the first prize, a boar's head, was cooked in the Hall, where, too, the first slice was cut off. Then the head, decorated with holly and ribbons, was borne aloft on a pitchfork to the Millfield. Often twenty wrestlers competed for the prize. Invariably the winner carried his trophy to the White Hart or King's Head, where he and his friends devoured it, washing it down with copious draughts of beer. Like many another Essex event, this sporting occasion became an excuse for excessive drinking and rowdyism with the inevitable result—public protests, then banning. The last contest took place on Christmas Day 1868.

Returning to the Bell, Upminster, we can reach North Ockendon, either by returning along St. Mary's Lane to Clay Tye Lane or by the more devious route through Corbets Tey. We follow the latter. Take a drink in the Huntsman and Hounds and you will soon be regaled with the popular explanation of the origin of the name Corbets Tey. Queen Elizabeth, it seems, passed this way, and feeling somewhat fatigued by the journey hailed a member of her retinue with the words, " Corbet, stay."

Corbets Tey has some interesting old buildings, but the most attractive is surely the Old Cottage. It gracefully fits into the curve of the road and one must regret that it is no longer an inn. This it ceased to be in 1901 after a century of service, when the last glass of beer was drawn by the licensee, Thomas Starr, and enjoyed by the local shoemaker, William Snell. During its years as an inn it bore the names Royal George, George and Dragon and plain George.

The road from Corbets Tey to White Posts Farm is a " rolling English road." The Old White Horse inn in North Ockendon stands at a crossroads of great antiquity, for here the Pilgrims' Way from North Essex to West Thurrock intersects the road from Bulphan to the church with its well of St. Cedd.

In South Ockendon the Royal Oak stands well back from the main road, overlooking a well-kept village green and a church of Norman foundation, the tower of which is one of the six round ones to be found in Essex.

The Royal Oak cannot claim such longevity, but it is certainly no upstart, for the north wing and about half the centre block were built before Columbus braved the Atlantic, and much of the remainder was standing when the Great Plague was ravaging England.

When the pilgrims were wending their way to Canterbury they passed by the Royal Oak, for it was not an inn in those days. Sir William Brandon, standard bearer to Henry VII on Bosworth Field, knew the building well, for his residence stood a few hundred yards down the chace.

Until fairly recently the interior of the Royal Oak differed in no way from any other " spit and sawdust " type of public-house. All traces of antiquity were thoroughly concealed by plasterboard. Now all is changed. The old has been revealed and the new has been made to blend with it. The rediscovered 500-year-old oak beams, now black as night, form an ideal background for the wealth of brass—coaching horns, tankards and horse brasses—which delights the eye and adds character to the room. Japanese prints, original watercolours, Wedgwood jugs, masonic tankards, beaten trays of exquisite eastern workmanship, a water-clock, fearsome-looking fish and numerous objects gathered from the four corners of the world feast the eye as you quench your thirst.

The richness of the saloon bar should not prevent the visitor from going into the public bar. Until a short while ago the cross-wing on the north side was a private residence. Since the Oak acquired it, all redundant accretions have been removed to reveal the stark but fascinating framework of a Tudor building, complete with king-post.

There are older inns in South Ockendon than the Royal Oak. In 1769 we had the King's Head, the Red Lion, the Crooked Billet and the Catherine Wheel, what time the Oak was a farmhouse called Eldertons after its occupier in the time of Charles II. By Benton's day the farm had been converted into a beer shop and the barns into cottages.

So the censure to be found in the " Quarter Sessions Order Book " for 1762 could not have applied to the Royal Oak: " Loose, idle, and disorderly persons . . . gathered on the Green at the pretended fair. . . . Some of which fairs are continued several days and great numbers of people stay there not only all day, but to very late hours in the night, and many unlawful games and plays, besides drinking and other debaucheries, are encouraged and carried on under pretence of meeting at such fairs to the great increase of vice and immorality and to the debauching and ruin of servants, apprentices, and other unwary people, and many riots, tumults and other disorders are occasioned thereby. For the preventing all such mischiefs and irregularities for the future, it is thought said fairs be henceforth absolutely suppressed."

To celebrate the coronation of Elizabeth II, the green was put to its time-honoured purpose—the place where all the villagers gathered to commemorate great events. With the ancient Oak and the even more ancient church as backcloths the whole colourful pageant of the village story was enacted.

From the green the pilgrims would have travelled southwards to the Mardyke and, crossing by the ancient ford, which was nearer the village than the present bridge, they would have proceeded to the right; but the modern pilgrim would do well to turn left after crossing the modern bridge in order to visit North Stifford, a delightful village with several thatched cottages. As one climbs the hill, the Dog and Partridge makes an attractive picture framed in fir trees. The present building is almost entirely rebuilt, but a Tudor fireplace is still retained inside. It is possible that this feature was part of the clockhouse that formerly stood on the site and gave its name to the lane opposite. It was Sir Thomas Gourney who lived beneath the clock, a sheriff of Essex in 1662.

If you do take a drink in the Dog and Partridge take heed of what happened to John: " 1767. Buried John—who died by excessive drinking of Gin, as appeared by the Coroner's Inquisition, this Tenth Day of June at the Sign of the Dog and Partridge."

The gin must have been stronger than the rum of a later landlord. The newspaper report of the case which took place at the Billericay petty sessions in 1831 is worth quoting in full.

" *A Rum Story*

" Mr. John Holt, landlord of the Dog and Partridge, Stifford, appeared to an information laid against him by Samuel Burrows, an officer, who seized upwards of a gallon of rum upon his premises which was 33 degrees below proof. On the defendant being asked whether he had any wish to interrogate Burrows, he rather irregularly replied that although the keg that the liquor was in had a seal affixed to the *cork* when taken away, there was none put upon the *tap, shrewdly* concluding that where there is a means of discharging there must be the same of receiving, but this idea did not *turn* much to the defendant's advantage. The seizure and disposal of the liquor seemed to be perfectly regular, and the bench declared the defendant to be guilty, which subjected him to the forfeiture of the spirits. No fine was sued for.

" Mr. Holt, by way of conclusion, observed it was a wonder Mr. Burrows never discovered the improper strength of his liquor before, as he (Mr. B.), had so frequently helped himself from the same fountain."

Both our stories have erred from the straight and narrow, so we had better make haste to follow once again the way of the pilgrims! Returning to the smithy near the Mardyke bridge, we take the left fork over the hill to the arterial road, then climb once more to Mill Lane. Now the river, with Kent beyond, is glimpsed. What a moment that must have been for the ancient pilgrim! Nowadays the view is somewhat obscured and the church, the pilgrims' landmark, is not seen until the London road is crossed. In medieval times its circular nave made it conspicuous, but of this structure only the foundations remain. Enlargement of the church took place in the thirteenth century. Surely a lonely church in the marshes would have been enlarged for one reason only—an increased pilgrim traffic.

There is no modern ferry near the church, but the presence of an inn, the Sun, until fairly recent times on nearby Stone Ness does suggest that the old ferry persisted even after the pilgrimages to Canterbury came to an end.

CHAPTER XVII

GRAYS TO RAINHAM

THE old High Street of Grays is fast disappearing, which is a pity, since it is the only part of the town which has age and character. There still clings around it the atmosphere of a seaport, which after all is not surprising, as it is still a port, although this fact is seldom realized by the thousands of shoppers who favour the new High Street beyond the level crossing. Drop into any of the inns in the old town and you are soon made aware that the river and the sea are not far away, for very evident are the shiny-peaked caps and the heavy blue serge favoured by ex-seamen. Conversation soon turns to things nautical. If you want to know the names of the famous Thames barges, or who skippered what, and when; if you want to know the tonnage of the *Orcades*, of the *Orion* or of their predecessors; if you want to know anything of river life today or for the last fifty years—then stand a pint to a thirsty old salt. The clear blue eyes twinkle as he recalls the vivid past, and the tales flow on as naturally and inevitably as the Thames itself.

A number of alterations have taken place recently in the old High Street. The Dutch House, built, it is believed, by one of the Dutchmen associated with the Thames dykes, was demolished a few years ago; the old White Hart has been replaced by a younger and more splendid offspring—and how odd the new-style building looks in such surroundings! Palin, whose delightfully prejudiced books on Thurrock still make interesting reading, would not have objected one bit if all the inns were removed. In 1871 he wrote, with some bitterness, that for its size Grays had more inns than any other town in England—and in his day they were all concentrated in the old High Street. And, as if that were not enough, Seabrooke's brewery was their companion for 100 years up to 1819. At the north end of the street stands the Bull inn. That it was a coaching inn is unmistakable, its central carriageway being still conspicuous.

On the Broadway, in the part of Grays known as Little Thurrock, is the Ship, the landlord of which has collected many fine maps and a variety of antiques. The extensive library of books dealing with Essex has, unfortunately, been dispersed.

West Thurrock has the Wharf inn, standing, as the name suggests, near the river and enjoying, therefore, all the advantages derived from such a position. If the view southwards has its attractions the same cannot be said of the view to the west. The jumble of masonry and derelict buildings has been mistaken frequently for a bombing disaster, a fact which has not escaped film directors, for scenes of the war film *The Guns of Loos* were actually shot on the site. The truth is that, although bombs did fall quite near during the Hitler war, the chaos is all that is left of an old cement factory, one of the original ones of Thurrock. Much is natural deterioration assisted by the depredations of youthful energy; the rest was dismantled by a building firm.

From the Wharf one should really continue up river by boat and alight on the King's Stairs in Purfleet. Their construction was authorized about 200 years ago " to enable watermen and villagers of Purfleet to avoid going through the ordnance grounds." The old ferry ante-dates their construction by several centuries. How long this north-south traffic has been going on it is impossible to say. It must not be forgotten, however, that the river has been travelled in other directions as well. Before the advent of railways and good roads it was quicker by river. Samuel Whitbread the brewer visited his country home in Purfleet by boat, and during the nineteenth century hundreds of Londoners made the trip in order to regale themselves in the Royal Hotel. Celebrities of stage and politics were also frequent visitors, for its whitebait suppers were quite famous.

Before its promotion to the dignity of hotel it was but the plain Bricklayers' Arms, an honest and direct allusion to its connection with the Bricklayers' Company of London, which, under Caleb Grantham, held extensive quarries in Purfleet.

The situation of the Royal Hotel is scarcely surpassed along the length of London's river. To sit in the forecourt or in the public right-of-way is to savour the delights of W. H. Davies's simple philosophy. Along the Thames ply ships from all over the world,

ROYAL OAK
NOCKENDON

THE THATCHERS
GREAT WARLEY

WELSH HARP

WALTHAM ABBEY

KING'S HEAD · CHIGWELL

each a symbol of adventure. Half-close your eyes and it is easy to imagine the wonderful pageant of the craft that have sailed the Thames—British coracles, Saxon long-boats, Tudor galleys and the rest—" liquid history."

Not far from the Royal is High House. A neighbouring field is still known as the Vineyard. A map of 1745 "performed" by Seth Partridge for Sir Henry Haman, Bart., and Sir Cranmer Harris, Kt., indicates that High House was known as the Vineyard in those days. Fobbing, Rayleigh and other places in south Essex also had their vineyards. Beyond these bare facts little else is known about them. Who planted them? When? What was the yield? When did they cease producing? The answers to all these questions are the same—we do not know. In the case of the Rayleigh vineyard we have a reference in the Domesday Book: " Manor—VI arpenni [less than an acre] of vineyard, which yielded XX barrels of wine in a good season. It was worth X pounds beside the wine."

One of the occupants of High House exemplified the preservative qualities of alochol. When the Rev. W. J. Hayes was rector of West Thurrock—we met him in Wivenhoe, you remember —he found it necessary to enlarge a vault some time in 1906. Breaking down a wall, he was surprised to find a leaden coffin. Overcome by curiosity, he rolled back some of the lead and was even more surprised to find inside the perfectly preserved body of a man. There was a considerable quantity of liquid inside the coffin, and Hayes, like a true researcher, decided to taste it. It was rum. Appropriately enough, the pickled man was a sailor— Nathaniel Grantham, ex-naval commander, buried in 1723. What an advertisement for the distillers!

Aveley stands a couple of miles inland from Purfleet. Signs of antiquity can still be discovered amid the tremendous flood of new building. The two oldest inns stand near the church. They are the Ship and the Crown and Anchor. The connection between the Ship and the church was not only geographical, for in 1813, for example, the parish decided to give a Christmas dinner to children and teachers of the Sunday school, and the place selected for the celebration was the Ship!

We do hope that this early introduction to an inn did not corrupt the Aveley children and cause the vestry as much concern as did the behaviour of some " persons " twenty years earlier. In that year the vestry passed a resolution: " Whereas it has been a custom for the Publicans and Alehousekeepers in the Parish of Aveley to permit persons to spend much time and money in their respective houses, and to permit and countenance drunkenness and disorderly proceedings on Sundays and on other days contrary to Law and good order, to the great discredit of this neighbourhood and contrary to all good government, it is mutually agreed and determined by the minister, churchwarden and overseers, as well as others of this parish to unite in suppressing and discountenancing such irregularities on this behalf, with as much severity as may be; and a copy of this determination is ordered to be delivered to every public house keeper in this parish."

We wonder if the vestry ever adjourned to the Harrow (which until 1850 stood opposite the church) to quench their thirst after reading this long resolution. If they did they might have met some "lunaticks"—members of the "Aveley Lunatick Clubb," which was founded in 1763. The declared purpose of this oddly named assembly was "to provide conversation and information for bored intellectual literates," and judging by the recruiting field—Wennington to Warley—the ennui was widespread. The club met on the first Monday after every full moon, members paid one shilling for dinner and anyone "fuddled, disguised in liquor or vulgarly speaking" was fined an additional shilling.

I do not know if any members came from Rainham, but it is certainly a place to get out of nowadays! Its most interesting building, the church, is nearly 1,000 years old—a sad criticism of the advance of civilization! Opposite the church stands the Phœnix, not as old or interesting as its neighbour, yet old enough to have been a coaching inn. The proprietor in the early years of the nineteenth century was also the postmaster. Carr's "Tilbury Coach" called at the house daily on its way to London at 9 p.m. and 6 a.m. How long the landlords acted as postmasters we do not know, but White's directory for 1848 stated that express mail could be sent by special horseman from the Phœnix. A daily omnibus also ran to London at this time, leaving Rainham in the morning.

The Phœnix is another of those inns which have introduced television into the bar.

"And what, sir, is your opinion concerning the introduction of television into our inns?"

"Sir, the practice is monstrous! One of the major delights of visiting an inn is to converse with friends and acquaintances.

Introduce a television apparatus and you toll the knell of fine conversation. Furthermore, the essential harmony which exists in our inns would be destroyed, for the viewers would be annoyed by the extraneous conversation and the conversationalists would resent the artificial competition emanating from the alien apparatus."

In 1951 the Murex company purchased the Three Crowns, which stood near the ancient Rainham ferry, so after many centuries of service as an alehouse and public-house it ceased to quench the thirst of the scores of visitors who used to converge at this point, either to gaze, like the young Raleigh of the painting, at the ships and the distant horizon or to use the age-old ferry. Records of 1200 state that it was the duty of Erith manor (on the Kent side) to maintain the ferry between the two counties. It is not certain if an inn of sorts existed as early as that, the earliest known record being dated 1556. The present building was erected about 1835 to replace one that had been burnt down the previous year. Not only the structure but the name, too, has changed through the centuries. Up to 1771 it was called the French Horn before it was changed to the Three Crowns, but, not unnaturally, it has also been known as the Ferry inn.

'CROSSKEYS'
DAGENHAM

CHAPTER XVIII

LONDON'S RIVER

L EAVING Rainham, we enter the conurbation of Greater London. Old inns there still are among the hundreds of new ones, but so overwhelmed are they by their surroundings that the seeker has to look long to find them, and when he has found them he longs to escape once more from the overpowering noise and dust to some quiet forest inn or to some remote marshland haven.

The very fact that there are still some inns left in this gigantic modern sprawl gives cause for surprise. In the case of Dagenham the reason is not hard to seek—the old village was left as a backwater when the new town sprang up nearby. It is not strange, therefore, to find the old church and the old inn standing on opposite sides of the road. Appropriately enough the inn is the Crosskeys—the sign of many inns found near churches. This, the oldest secular building in Dagenham, is a fine example of a fifteenth-century timber-framed house, and was built, it is believed, by one of the Comyns family. Like many another inn of ancient foundation, it started life as a private residence, not becoming an inn until about 1700, when one John French was landlord. When, in 1708, he sold it to John Gull, it was termed " all that messuage or tenement called or known by the name or signe of the *Queens Head* . . . lying & being in Daggenham over against the church there."

Some time during that same century the name was changed to the Crosskeys. Of course, the inn has been enlarged during its long life, and regular repairs have kept it in good condition, but in 1952 it was noticed that the ravages of the death-watch beetle were so extensive that immediate and drastic action had to be taken to combat the menace. The measures proved successful and the old inn is fit once more for another 500 years of active service.

When James Fisher, landlord of the Crosskeys, appeared before the magistrate between 1744 and 1780, the sureties he provided were Joshua St. Pere of the Chequers, Thomas Creswell of the Bull, Daniel Dossiter of the White Horse, Abraham Miller of the Sheep Coat and William Cox of the Rose and Crown.

Of these only the Bull and the Chequers still remain, but their appearance has changed. The former still stands in Old Dagenham and bears some resemblance to an old print of the original inn. The Chequers is unmistakable. You can find it—quite easily!—on Ripple Road, since its black-and-white checky decoration proclaims its name from a distance. Incidentally, the sign of the chequer-board is among the oldest of inn signs. Examples have been found at Pompeii, and in some ancient inns in this country; at Corsham in Wiltshire, for example, a small chequer pattern is painted on the wall near the entrance.

To associate the name of Elizabeth Fry, the great prison reformer, with a Dagenham inn seems odd. The connection is indeed but slight, but not without interest. Elizabeth's husband, Joseph, had bought the Gulf with land and cottages and held it until he failed in business. It still remained in the family after this event, his wife's brother, Samuel Gurney, buying the lease. Elizabeth spent many a happy holiday on Thamesside, as we learn from her " journals." On August 21, 1821, she had to shelter in the old Chequers during a violent thunderstorm when she was returning from a religious meeting in Becontree. One farm worker was killed by lightning and Elizabeth wrote: " This awful event produced a very serious effect in the neighbourhood . . . the relations of the young man and the other men in the neighbourhood came to meet us in the little Methodist meeting house, which ended in one more rather large public meeting."

On Ripple Road—that road of apt name which winds from Dagenham in the direction of London via Barking—is a plain inn with the unusual name of the Ship and Shovel. Gurney Benham believed that there was some connection between Sir Clowdisley Shovel and the inn. At one time Sir Clowdisley's portrait hung inside the inn. Let us hope that it was in better taste than the monument erected to his memory in Westminster Abbey, for as Admiral of the Fleet in the reign of William and Mary he certainly deserved better. As Trevelyan points out, English sea-power as a factor in the downfall of Louis XIV has seldom been given its full credit. With a diplomat like William and a soldier of the calibre of Marlborough this is understandable. The admiral was not in their class, but the fleet under his command played an important part not only in waging war but in lending support to William's diplomacy.

Sir Clowdisley's bravery is unquestioned. There is a family tradition that he even conveyed important dispatches in his mouth when swimming under enemy fire. That he faced the storms and tempests of mighty seas in the course of his career is obvious. How ironic, then, that he should meet his death at the hands of a woman—and an unknown countrywoman at that! When his ship was wrecked off the Scillies, Sir Clowdisley was washed ashore and his all-but-lifeless body was discovered by an islander, who noticed the emerald ring he was wearing and committed murder to gain possession of it. This she admitted years later when she lay dying. When the admiral's body was discovered it was conveyed to Plymouth, where it was embalmed and then borne to London and laid to rest in the abbey.

Not far from this spot, somewhere on the levels near Dagenham Breach, was fought, on March 13, 1820, one of those fierce and bloody bare-knuckle contests which we have noted before. The Ship and Shovel was the house of call that day and Parish and Hadbrook were the contestants. After forty-one rounds of merciless battering, Hadbrook failed to come up to " toe the line," so Parish was declared the winner.

In Barking itself we find another Bull inn, one which was mentioned in a deed of the fourteenth century: " . . . *tectum vel hospitium vocatum le Bole* . . ." As we have already noted, old inns under this sign are seldom associated with the animal. The bull referred to is the papal *bulla*. We have mentioned, too, that monasteries provided the traveller with accommodation, that is they served the same purpose as our hotels. As the demands for hospitality increased, religious houses found it necessary to build hostels outside their walls. The Bull inn, Barking, was one such hostel and was attached to the celebrated Barking nunnery until the dissolution. Then, in 1636, it was sold to St. Margaret's Hospital, Westminster, for the sum of one shilling!

The last two inns to note on the Essex Thameside are lost in the maze of streets of West Ham. Ye Olde Spotted Dog is comparatively easy to find, since it is in Upton Lane, near West Ham

Park. You will no doubt be surprised when you see it, for here, in the heart of a great bustling town, is a village inn. It is a six-teenth-century structure built on the H plan, with two gables facing the street. Parts of the house are of timber and the roofs are tiled. Seen from the opposite side of the road through the pretty trees growing in front of it, the Spotted Dog makes an attractive picture.

Some of the inside timbers look rather suspiciously pseudo. At present the alleged ancient beams support basketed jars, and it is very unlikely that they could support anything heavier. Even if the beams are false there is nothing false about the general plan of the interior, for here we have preserved for us the essential layout of a sixteenth-century house—a feat not to be taken lightly in a town which has preserved so little that is truly old.

During the Great Fire of London the city fathers held their meetings in this inn, but the claim that Charles II knighted the loin of beef here is not supported by any evidence. Two other inns in Epping Forest make the same claim!

Our last inn on London's river is the Adam and Eve. It is hidden away near the end of Manor Lane. Why it is called the Adam and Eve it is impossible to say, for any surroundings less like paradise would be hard to find—cobbled streets, bare brick walls, factories, chimney-stacks, railways. So in the midst of this stark industrial scene the inn is a pleasant, and unexpected, oasis.

But this inn has a story which takes us back to the days of woods and green fields, features that even Adam and Eve would have recognized. Who would dream that on this stark spot there once stood a monastery? It was the abbey of Stratford Langthorne, founded in the year 1135 for the monks of the order of Savigny. Subsequently it became a Cistercian community.

Chaucer himself must have known it, for from his rooms on the city gate he would have been able to see it. His prioress, you will remember, spoke French after the school of Stratford-atte-Bowe.

The monks were responsible for maintaining the famous bridge at Bow in a good state of repair—a bridge, incidentally, which is supposed to be the first arched stone bridge to be built in Essex. About the only remains of the abbey are a few thirteenth-century window stones in a modern wall near the inn. Benton wrote of a stone arch in the inn garden, but that has disappeared. Gone, too, are the coffin, the seal, the coins and the urns dug up in an adjoining field over a century ago (the field has also gone!), and nothing remains of the former moat.

A footbridge alongside the Adam and Eve crosses many railway lines. What sonnet would Wordsworth have written standing on this bridge gazing at the surrounding scene through the iron girders? Or what would Omar Khayyam have said—" That Paradise is Wilderness enow "?

SPOTTED DOG · WEST HAM

CHAPTER XIX

INNS OF THE FOREST

LIKE Defoe, we cross the Lea at Bow and travel northwards to Leytonstone, with the Green Man standing near the church. There are many theories concerning the origin of this widespread sign. One connects it with Robin Hood and a number of signs display this popular hero; another is much more involved. When in former days the aristocracy absented themselves for a long period from one of their numerous mansions, the head gamekeeper was allowed to take in guests for his own profit. When eventually he quit the service of his master, he was so enamoured of the joys of inn-keeping that he set up on his own and, in grateful thanks for his previous post, he adopted the sign of the Green Man—the colour of his former livery.

Whatever the truth may be, the sign is not an inappropriate one to display in Leytonstone, for we feel that we are approaching Epping Forest. Dick Turpin and his gang must have enjoyed the same feeling too, if for different reasons, for they knew that when they arrived at the Green Man from London they were half-way to their forest hide-out and comparative safety. Legends of the highwaymen have grown up around the inn. Formerly one of the rooms contained a chest large enough to conceal several persons. The false bottom gave access to a room below, in the floor of which was a trap-door opening on a short passage leading to the forest. Several old pistols and other relics have been found in the inn.

Not all the famous callers at the Green Man have been notorious. Daniel Defoe and the philosopher Locke were visitors, but it is a fact that men and events of a criminal nature are the ones which are remembered longest. Take the case of Christopher Layer for example. He, his friend Mr. Stephen Lynch, and Mr. Layer's servant were on their way to dine with Lord North and Grey at Epping, but having been delayed they decided to have dinner at

121

the inn. While waiting for their meal to be prepared they talke
of many things, some of which should have been left well alone
for certain opinions expressed in the quiet intimacy of the hostelr
led to a case of high treason.

To quote the indictment dated October 31, 1722: " Christophe
Layer, Esq., late of the Parish of St. Andrews, Holborn, bein
seduced by the instigation of the Devil as a false traitor agains
our said Lord, the King, withdrawing that cordial love and tru
and due obedience, fidelity, and allegiance which every subjec
of our said Lord should and ought to bear, and designing with a
your might traitorously to change and alter the government o
this Kingdom, to depose and deprive and bring to death and
destruction our Sovereign Lord the King at Leytonstone, in th
County of Essex, you did falsely, maliciously, devilishly, an
traitorously compass, imagine and intend, our said Lord the Kin
to depose and deprive, and that you the said Christopher Laye
did with divers other false traitors at Leytonstone, aforesaid, mee
propose, consult, conspire, consent, agree, to move, raise and lev
insurrection and that at Leytonstone aforesaid, you did publish
certain malicious, seditious, and traitorous writing," etc.

To cut a long story short, it seems that while waiting for thei
steak Christopher Layer disclosed the whole plot—to seize th
Tower and to capture, with the aid of the Army, Lord Cadoga
and the king.

The only evidence advanced was provided by Lynch, who
admitted that his understanding of the paper shown him by Laye
was slight, but nevertheless declared that it carried detailed plan
for carrying the treason into effect. Layer was imprisoned in th
Tower and on Wednesday, October 3, he was taken in chains t
Westminster. After a long trial, he was hanged, drawn and quartered

North of Leytonstone there are a number of good roads whic
could be followed with profit. If you are a Dickens admirer th
road to Ongar cannot be ignored, for at Chigwell is the Maypol
of *Barnaby Rudge*. You will not find this sign, however, for th
actual inn is the King's Head. Even if you are not an admirer o
the great novelist you should still visit the inn for its own sak
In spite of the proximity of London, Chigwell is still a delightfu
village and the inn, church and ancient grammar school ar
pleasantly grouped amid lovely trees.

Perhaps the best approach to the King's Head is along Rodin

Lane, then at the end of this tree-lined avenue can be seen the Dickens hall. The main building is south of this, and although largely of the seventeenth century has, as Pevsner puts it, " been much vamped up." I shall not dare to describe the building—when the writings of the master are at hand—but the reader should make allowances for his verbal exuberance.

" An old building, with more gable ends than a lazy man would care to count on a sunny day; huge zig-zag chimneys, out of which it seemed as though even smoke could not choose but come in more than naturally fantastic shapes, imported to it in its tortuous passage; and vast stables, gloomy, ruinous, and empty. The place was said to have been built in the days of King Henry the Eighth, and there was a legend, not only that Queen Elizabeth had slept there one night while upon a hunting excursion, to wit, in a certain oak-panelled room with a deep bay window, but that next morning, while standing on a mounting block before the door with one foot in the stirrup, the Virgin Monarch had then and there boxed and cuffed an unlucky page for some neglect of duty. . . .

" Whether these, and many other stories of a like nature, were true or untrue, the Maypole was really an old house, a very old house, perhaps as old as it claimed to be, and perhaps older, which will sometimes happen with houses of an uncertain, as with ladies of a certain, age. Its windows were old diamond pane lattices, its floors were sunken and uneven, its ceilings blackened by the hand of time, and heavy with massive beams. . . . With its overhanging stories, drowsy little panes of glass, and front bulging out and projecting over the pathway, the old house looked as if it were nodding in its sleep. . . . The bricks of which it was built had originally been a deep dark red, but had grown yellow and dis-coloured like an old man's skin; the sturdy timbers had decayed like teeth; and here and there the ivy, like a warm garment to comfort it in its age, wrapped its green leaves closely round the time-worn walls."

And so on. For the full account go to the book, for there is no one like Dickens for conjuring up the atmosphere of an English inn.

Dickens loved Chigwell. To his friend Forster he wrote: " Chig-well, my dear fellow, is the greatest place in the world. Name your day of going. Such a delicious old inn opposite the church—such a lovely ride—such beautiful forest scenery—such an out-of-the-way rural place—such a sexton! I say again, name your day."

" His promise was exceeded by our enjoyment," wrote Forster
" and his delight in the double recognition of himself and of
Barnaby by the landlord of the nice old inn far exceeded any prid
he would have taken in what the world thinks the highest sort of
honour."

The King's Head is, without a doubt, the most picturesque inn
throughout the forest region, an honour not difficult to attain
however, for it is a surprising fact that very few of the inns to be
found in this delightful countryside are outstandingly attractive
Many are large brick buildings of the type associated with railway
hotels. One can only despair at the shortsightedness of the builders—
for they were certainly not architects.

Not far from Chingford station—the end of the line and a con
venient springboard for jumping off into the forest—is the huge
Royal Forest hotel. Standing demurely, but not entirely abashed
alongside is the picturesque building known as Queen Elizabeth'
Hunting Lodge. It was known as a " standing," a place where
people stood to watch the hunt. Now it is a museum with a very
fine staircase, which the queen is said to have climbed on her
pony, a feat which would not have been difficult, for the treads are
low.

A good hotel needs no forest, but a hinterland as interesting as
that of the Royal Forest hotel is, of course, an asset. In the woods
around the beautiful Connaught Waters are many rare prizes for
the keen naturalist, but you need not be an expert to enjoy wandering
in the delightful groves of oak and hornbeam which radiate from
Grimstone's Oak.

The signs of the forest inns reflect the larger denizens of the
woodlands—the Reindeer, the Roebuck and the Baldfaced Stag
for example. This last inn, to be found in Buckhurst Hill, is a large
modern hotel, but its own sign is dimmed by the multitude of red
pegasi—animals not indigenous to Epping Forest!—displayed
outside the neighbouring garage and petrol station.

The Roebuck, too, is a large hotel, but preserves something of its
forest associations by standing well back from the high road
Although most of the building is of recent origin, a little of the
eighteenth century can still be spotted in one corner.

In the early nineteenth century the Roebuck was the scene of
the " Essex Stag Hunt," a farcical affair, the main purpose of
which seems to have been to provide an excuse for an orgy of

eating and drinking. The hunt was extremely popular with Londoners, and their behaviour was satirized by artist and writer, and it must be admitted that the scope was considerable. At one time, though, the hunt was respectable and dignified and was attended by the Lord Mayor of London and his aldermen, " baronets and butchers, dandies and dustmen, tailors and tinkers, nobocracy and snobocracy " who came by " coach and chaise, whisky and cart, gig and waggon, hunter and hack, horse and ass."

At first the stag was brought on Easter Monday from Buckhurst Hill to Fairmead, and there released. Sometimes the run was good, providing much excitement, but at other times, when the tame quarry refused to show any pleasure in being chased through the greenwood, the hunt had to be abandoned and the animal returned to the paddock in Buckhurst Hill, to be given an opportunity at a later date to play the game! When the hunt was called off, " woeful was Whitechapel, melancholy the men of Mile End, sorrow sighed in Shoreditch, and Gracechurch Street groaned in grief."

But why should the cockney huntsmen suffer so? Why not guarantee the success of the hunt and thus make every Easter Monday memorable? After all, the visitors were not expected to chase the animal; a look was all that was demanded. So in the final decadent days the stag was paraded around the forest inns and displayed at so much per head. The solution was approved; the animal was viewed and the drinking was scarcely interrupted! By 1860 the farcical hunt was more or less dead, but it managed to struggle on for another twenty years or so before finally expiring.

Another well-known forest festivity is commemorated in the Fairlop Oak inn. This was the Fairlop fair, which enjoyed great popularity from the early part of the eighteenth century until the late nineteenth.

Mr. Daniel Day, affectionately known as " Good " Day, was a prosperous maker of engines, blocks and pumps in Wapping. Every year, on the first Friday in July, he would set out with a number of his friends to collect his Essex rents. The task completed, they would all picnic in the shade of the Fairlop Oak, a huge tree whose branches covered about 300 square feet of ground.

About 1725 these beanfeasts—literally—attracted the attention of many people outside Day's circle of friends, and it was not long before booths were set up to cater for the newcomers. Soon the fair became an annual event, and strangely enough Daniel and his cronies still held their beanfeasts regardless of the increasing crowds. No doubt he enjoyed the celebrity. This is fair to assume, for his progress to the fair was anything but self-effacing. Scorning plebeian progress in a carriage, he and his friends sat like naval heroes in a fully rigged boat which was hauled by six stalwart horses. A band completed the " crew " and, in case their music failed to give sufficient warning of the approach of the cavalcade, outriders, clad like the postilion in blue and gold, rode on in front. Starting at Barking Creek, the procession went by way of Stratford, Forest Gate, Manor Park, Ilford, Fulwell Hatch and the Bald Hind to Fairlop.

Day died in 1767 and was buried in a coffin made out of a branch of his beloved oak. His death did not halt the Fairlop fair or the annual procession, and even the " death " of the oak in 1820 had little effect on the celebration.

Publicans along the route benefited from the procession, and many displayed a notice proclaiming that the boat stopped at their houses. Arriving at the stump of the tree, the procession marched round it three times, then returned to the Roebuck, the Maypole or the Bald Hind.

The Disafforesting Act of 1852 dealt the death blow to Fairlop fair. The traditional site was barred, and although other places were tried none was as successful as the original, and in 1899 the fair was held for the last time.

In Loughton, a left fork takes us along the Earl's Path to the Robin Hood, a large modern hotel with a " Robin Hood Service Station " as its neighbour, where, presumably, bows, arrows and quarterstaffs can be serviced! From this point delightful paths lead into the forest in all directions. A great favourite is the one to High Beech, for when the walker arrives at this spot his wants are catered for whether they be æsthetic, historical or athletic. Dominating the scene is the King's Oak. Stand in front of it and away over the grassy banks and through the trees you can see the gleaming tower of Waltham Abbey. It was near this same spot, we are told, that Tennyson heard the bells of the abbey—the sound of which moved him to write that poem expressing the deep yearning of our age—" Ring in the thousand years of peace."

Somewhere beneath a great oak, in this neighbourhood too, sat Henry VIII on the day that Anne Boleyn was executed. He did not want to remain in London, yet he wanted to be near enough to

ear the cannon in the Tower that was to be fired to announce
hat the deed was accomplished. When he did hear the report,
Henry exclaimed: " The day's work is done. Uncouple the hounds,
and let us follow the sport."

Henry's sport was not the same as today's. Behind the King's
Oak you will now find a swimming pool and, amazingly, a speedway
racing stadium!

There is one fact concerning Epping Forest which everyone
knows—that Dick Turpin " worked " there. Naturally he would
have a hide-out, and this is conveniently provided beneath a small
inn a few hundred yards from the King's Oak. Dick's cave is a wet
hole about eleven feet long by about seven feet high. Why this
unsavoury excavation should have such a terrific attraction is
difficult to understand, but then the whole remarkable hero-
worship of this murderous outlaw is also difficult to understand.
He was an unmitigated rogue and cut-throat, with, as far as can
be determined, no redeeming features, yet the adulation with
which he is regarded stops only just this side of the angels. Of
course, Harrison Ainsworth is largely responsible for this moral
somersault. In his book *Rookwood* he created a figure which bears
little resemblance to the real Turpin.

Dick Turpin was born in the Bell, Hempstead, in north Essex,
in 1705, although it must not be assumed that he was a product
of his environment—a great number of his contemporary rogues
were sons of the manse! The young Dick became apprenticed to a
butcher in Whitechapel. His apprenticeship completed, he married
Esther Palmer, of East Ham. It was at this time that he first turned
to crime—or perhaps we should say that his criminal acts were
first discovered. Like all rogues, he thought that he had found a
short cut to wealth by, in his case, obtaining supplies of meat
without the owner's consent. His master discovered the practice
and, not unnaturally, discharged him.

Like many another criminal in similar circumstances he sought
revenge. He stole two of his former employer's cattle and offered
the hides for sale in the market in Waltham Abbey. The crime was
detected, but Dick managed to slip out through a back window of
his house when the constables were knocking on his front door to
serve him with a warrant for his arrest.

In an earlier chapter we noted that the Thames flats were a
haunt of smugglers in bygone days, and it was there that he now

fled to join a gang which operated between Plaistow and Hadleigh Castle. The *Newgate Calendar* points out that any success he enjoyed was short-lived, since the customs officers, " by one successful stroke, deprived him of his ill-gotten gains."

He now returned to Epping Forest, where, to increase his " ill-gotten gains " he combined deer-stealing with house-breaking. The latter practice yielded more profit and required less physical effort. He and his partner chose a lonely cottage. One of them knocked at the door and the occupant, seeing only one person outside, opened the door wide. At this both robbers rushed in and terrified the victim into revealing where the money was hidden. In Loughton £400 was obtained in this manner from an old lady. At first she refused to divulge the hiding place, but when the gallant highwayman held her over the fire she, not unnaturally, changed her mind. On another occasion the two thieves beat a forest keeper to death and made off with about 140 guineas.

The gang increased in size and brutal robberies became more frequent and widespread. After one particularly beastly episode a substantial reward was offered for the arrest of the gang. One of the number, attracted by the money, double-crossed two of his fellow cut-throats and they ended up on the gibbet. This even convinced Turpin, not that crime did not pay but that there was no safety in numbers, so he left the gang and worked on his own for a while.

Once on the Cambridge road he held up a well-dressed man, who turned out to be no other than the notorious highwayman King. The latter pointed out that dog did not eat dog and suggested joining forces. The combination proved a great success, so much so that no inn in the forest dared to accommodate them. Loath to leave the security of Epping, they made their home, it is said, in the cave already referred to. The position was ideal, since they could see the road without being seen and they were provided with food by Dick's wife, who lived in Sewardstone.

On one of their trips to London they met a Mr. Major near the Green Man, Leytonstone, and forced him to exchange horses. But Mr. Major preferred his own horse and, desiring to get it back, circulated a description. This must have been accurate, since he was soon informed that a horse tallying with his description could be found in Whitechapel at the sign of the Red Lion. Turpin's brother, who had come to buy the animal, was found in possession

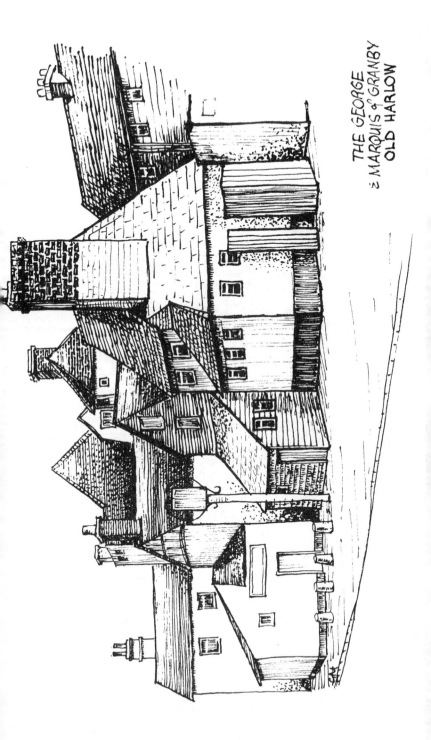

THE GEORGE
& MARQUIS of GRANBY
OLD HARLOW

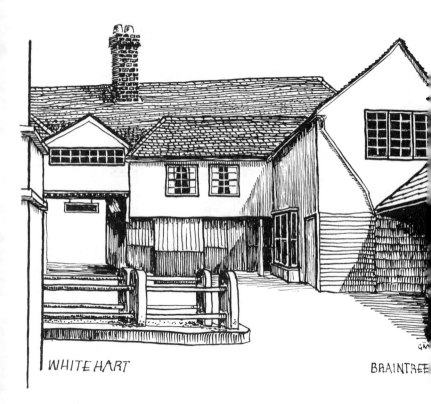

WHITE HART   BRAINTREE

of a stick bearing Mr. Major's name and consequently he was arrested. He was promised his freedom if he revealed the whereabouts of his infamous brother. Acting on his advice, the constables went to Red Lion Street. Their approach was noted by King, who promptly levelled his gun at them. It failed to go off, so King called upon Dick to shoot. For some unknown reason Dick's aim was bad and his bullet struck King. Turpin did not wait to note the result but rode off at top speed.

His Epping Forest cave was no longer a safe hide-out, so after eluding the bloodhounds that had been set on his trail he decided to leave the district altogether. He went to Yorkshire.

There he mixed with the gentry, but money was necessary to maintain this new social standing and this Turpin obtained by selling horses. They were not his own, of course. He stole them in Lincolnshire and sold them in Yorkshire, an arrangement which worked well. Strangely enough, it was a comparatively trifling incident that led to his downfall. Returning from a hunt one day, he shot a cock belonging to his landlord. His companion was amazed at such behaviour and said so. He was even more amazed when Turpin threatened to shoot him for saying such a thing. The companion was extremely piqued, but deemed it wiser to say nothing then but to report the matter to the landlord at the earliest opportunity. Turpin was arrested and inquiries followed. It was not long before the horse-stealing was uncovered, and the criminal was moved to York Castle. His true identity, however, was unknown, since he had adopted his wife's maiden name of Palmer.

This was the signature he wrote on the letter he sent to his brother in which he requested a " character." The brother would not pay the postage, so the letter was returned to the post office. Here the handwriting was recognized by Dick's former schoolmaster and he informed the magistrate of his discovery. A journey to York confirmed the identity of the prisoner. There was now no doubt how Turpin would end. He met his death quite gallantly. Clad in a new fustian frock and a new pair of pumps, he was hanged on April 10, 1739.

I have dealt at some length with Turpin, since wherever we go in Essex we are regaled with tales of his adventures. According to legend he used dozens of inns as places of concealment, and present-day landlords need very little encouragement to show the inquirer the bed the highwayman slept in, the cupboard leading to a trap-door, the escape chest with the false bottom, the very gun with which he killed King—and so on. Most of the tales can be discounted, but there are so many stories told that it is extremely difficult to separate truth from legend.

The old-time relics on show in the bar of Turpin's Cave inn are claimed as Turpin's own, but no proof is offered. Among them are to be found flint-lock pistols, two huge locks, a cutlass with scabbard, and handcuffs. On the wall hang some dark-brown prints illustrating various escapades of Dick Turpin.

From High Beech—or Beach (and, incidentally, there is no better way of starting an argument in the Epping inns than supporting one or other of these spellings)—there is a pleasant walk to the Wake Arms, which stands near a busy forest crossroads. The continuous traffic in front of this inn is hardly consistent with the popular conception of what stirs down in forests. Fortunately, however, escape into the forest is easy and the walk to the top of Claypit Hill is among the prettiest imaginable. Along the way grow representatives of all the forest trees. Because we are dealing in superlatives Wake Valley pond must be mentioned, since forest connoisseurs regard it as the loveliest of the large areas of water to be found in their domain.

The Wake Arms itself is a long, low building, the straightness of its roof broken by attractive flower boxes.

Eastwards a road leads to Theydon Bois, with its Bull inn; westwards another road goes by Woodridden Hill, Skillet Hill and sweet-named Honey Lane to Waltham Abbey. In a town as old as Waltham Abbey we expect to find old inns clustered around the abbey, and we are not disappointed. The oldest of all is thought to have been at one time a religious guest house. This is the Welsh Harp, situated in the market square. It is a fifteenth-century building with an archway leading to the precincts. It has been suggested that at the entrance to this thoroughfare stood the original lich-gate.

Shades of Cranmer, Thomas Fuller and Foxe haunt the precincts, and no doubt these worthies used the old archway on occasions. In a neighbouring house Cranmer " struck the keynote of the Reformation and claimed for the Word of God that supremacy which had been usurped by the Popes for centuries." Fuller was vicar here a century later, and it was in Waltham Abbey, too, that

Foxe wrote that book which has been quoted from time to time in this present work—his *Book of Martyrs*.

Near the abbey stands the Cock, a sign dating back to at least 1599, for it is on record that " John Broadly of the Cock " was married in the February of that year.

The Crown in the neighbouring cattle market is not so ancient, but it is not lacking in interest. Few inns in Essex have cattle pens within a yard or two of their front doors. Market day is, of course, the best day to visit the Crown. Outside are the noise, sound and smell of cattle, while inside the farmers forgather and discuss in language of the earth earthy the merits of their cattle, and recount in rich detail all that has happened on their farms since the last market day.

" Julie, 1612, Margarett the daughter of Edward of Cestrehunt, was buried 26 daye, dwelling at signe of Ye Olde Swanne in Waltham Cross." An inn that was " olde " in 1612 is certainly worth a visit, even though it happens to be in the next county of Hertfordshire. The Four Swans, to give it its present name, stands where the road from the abbey joins Ermine Street. Travellers along the old Roman road see from afar a beam spanning the road on which float four large swans.

On Ermine Street itself stands the best remaining example of the twelve crosses which were erected on those spots where the body of Queen Eleanor was rested on its way from Nottinghamshire to Westminster Abbey. There is even a tradition that the body was placed in the inn overnight.

Salmon the historian believed that the Four Swans was the original manor house of the Earl of Richmond, a natural son of Henry VIII.

It is only to be expected that a hostelry occupying such an important site should have been a coaching inn.

We must not be lured farther into Hertfordshire by such tempting bait as the Four Swans. Time now to return to our starting point at the Wake Arms, then to proceed by Jack's Hill and Coppice Row to Theydon Bois. In the angle where the severe-looking new road meets the old road stands the attractive Bull inn. It is best admired viewed some distance from the front, then the big black bull which decorates the façade stands out in all its might. The west side of the house is the oldest, dating from Tudor days, but the whole building is scheduled as an ancient monument. A recent proposal to take down the building and rebuild it on the other side of the new main road was turned down, and all admirers of the Bull breathed a sigh of relief.

About two miles away in Abridge is the White Hart. This inn was probably the one referred to by John Taylor the Water Poet in 1636, although he does not mention it by name. White's *Essex Gazetteer and Directory* for 1848 stated that a coach left every morning, Sundays excepted, from London and when it returned in the evening continued to Dunmow.

It would be pleasant to wander along the Roding valley, but we must save that pleasure for later. Instead we return to Theydon Bois, then proceed by Piercing Hill to Epping town. We meet the forest road at Bell Common, on which stands the Bell, a most attractive inn well back from the road. In summer time its tea gardens are pleasant and popular.

Epping is a town of inns, and all except one are on the south-east side of the High Street—the exception being the Black Lion. Long ago, in 1651, it was known as the Black Boy and in those days it brewed its own beer. The sign was changed in 1755. Of all the inns in the town this was the only one which was allowed to remain open all night to cater for the drivers of the London-bound haycarts.

The architecture of the inns is varied and not without interest. Coachways are common; signs mostly depict animals and there seems to be a conscious pride in displaying them. Both the White Hart and the Swan have their signs worked in plaster relief on the front gables. Next door to the White Lion is a smithy proclaiming its business by displaying gigantic horseshoes on its weatherboarded front. In the heyday of coach travel we can well imagine the anvil music and the brilliant showers of sparks that must have brightened the numerous smithies of the town. The George and Dragon is pleasantly shuttered, but the most attractive inns are undoubtedly the Cock, with its gay chanticleer perky above the front porch, and Ye Olde Thatched Cottage, the latter belying its sign by being roofed with tiles and by being anything but a cottage! Indeed these two inns occupy a greater length of the High Street than any other two buildings in the town! The Water Poet mentioned the Cock, but its neighbour is not much younger. Both are well appointed and provide fare comparable with that of the best London hotels.

In coaching days the principal inn of the town was the Epping

Place inn. Chapman and André recorded it on their map of 1722, although it was not an inn at that time if we are to believe the "Gentleman" who in his *History of Essex* gave the date of 1760 for its conversion, remarking at the same time that it was "much frequented." This date indicates that the change must have taken place shortly after the widow of Lord North and Grey sold the property to Edward Conyers, of Copped Hall. There can be little doubt that it became an inn to help cater for the considerable traffic on the Newmarket road—about twenty coaches a day, as well as wagons and private carriages. The building, formerly called Winchelsea House, had been constructed about 1635, at the time when Lord Grey de Werk bought the manor of Epping.

Epping Place inn was "much frequented" by many celebrities, including royalty. A visitor to the inn at the turn of the eighteenth century would have been surprised at the size of some of the doors, made, it would seem, to accommodate a giant. In fact that was the reason! The giant was Patrick O'Brien, reputed to be eight feet four inches in height. In 1801 at the age of thirty-seven he died at the inn, where he had been living for a number of years.

From 1769 the Epping and Ongar Turnpike Trust held its meetings in the Epping Place inn, but was forced to discontinue the practice in 1844 when the proprietor found it necessary to dispose of the coaching and posting business. The importance of the inn up to this time can be gauged by this sale, at which forty-two horses, complete with harness, coaches and equipment, were sold. After this event life at the inn became uninteresting and it was inevitable that it would close down. This it did in 1848. William Stokes had been the first licensee and the inn was in the possession of that same Stokes family until a Caroline Stokes disposed of its contents and had it converted into two dwelling places.

Near the Black Lion which we noted on the north-east side of Epping High Street there once stood another inn called the Black Dog. When its services became redundant it was converted into a grocery store and has remained one to this day. As an inn it had no claim to fame, and would scarcely be remembered but for the fact that one of its proprietors in its soberer days after becoming a grocery was Henry Doubleday. He was quite an exceptional grocer—being an entomologist and ornithologist of distinction. Before removing the shutters from the grocery windows in the morning he used to hurry along to the forest and there smear the trunks of numerous trees with a sticky substance of his own devising. After replacing his shutters in the evening he again went to the forest to collect the specimens which, attracted by the smell of the bait, had ventured too near for their freedom. The insects, grubs, etc., were then taken back to his shop, where they were dissected, catalogued and classified.

Doubleday was no dabbling amateur. His *Synonimic List of British Lepidoptera*, issued between 1847 and 1850, was highly regarded by experts, and later classifiers acknowledged their debt to it. Darwin, in his *Descent of Man*, made several references to Doubleday's work, and respected in particular his researches on moths.

Epping might seem to have many inns for a smallish town, but in the nineteenth century there were crowded into the half-mile of the High Street some twenty-two inns! Most of them had sprung up when the great highway between London and the eastern counties was built in the early seventeenth century. The rapid growth is indicated by the fact that in 1631 there were only five innholders and ten victuallers in Epping, but by 1681 when the road was completed there were twenty-four innholders. This number increased every year to cater for the increasing number of coaches and travellers. The prosperity of Epping reached its height in the early nineteenth century with twenty-five coaches a day stopping in the town to change horses or to allow refreshment for the jolted passengers, before dashing away again to the sound of post horn and galloping hooves.

In 1865 the railway reached Epping; the colourful coaches with their noise and glamour became redundant. The number of inns diminished accordingly and the main street, which at one time was almost all inns on the south side, adapted itself to the changing conditions and now the present-day traveller has only a dozen or so to choose from.

In which of the inns of Epping town did the great diarist stay one night?

" So we went to our Inn, and after eating of something and kissed the daughter of the house, she being very pretty, we took leave, and so that night, the road pretty good but the weather rainy, to Epping, where we sat and played a game of cards, and after supper and some merry talk with a plain bold maid of the house, we went to bed. Up in the morning then to London through the forest, where we found the way good." Need I ask which diarist?

It is with reluctance that we leave the forest with its inns, its lore and its beauty. The road northwards, however, is not unpleasant, and soon brings us to Latton, with its Sun and Whalebone. The attractive sign displays two whales disposed symmetrically on either side of a sun resplendent. On each side of the sign-post is a huge whalebone curving upwards towards the sign. The bones are obviously much older than the present inn, but whence they came no one knows. Did they come from the Thames? Many tales are told of whales becoming stranded in that river. Or did they come from Dagenham? Defoe, in his *Tour Throughout the Whole Island of Britain*, wrote: " . . . and passing that part of the great forest which we now call Hainault Forest, came into that which is now the great road a little this side the Whalebone, a place in the road so called because a rib-bone of a great whale which was taken in the river of Thames the same year that Oliver Cromwell died, 1658, was fixed there for a monument of that monstrous creature, it being at first about eight-and-twenty foot long." (Perhaps it should be pointed out that Defoe is inaccurate regarding the date. The Whalebone is mentioned in a forest perambulation of 1640.)

A road sign informs us that we are approaching Harlow. The new town has one inn to date, the Essex Skipper, opened at 12 noon on Wednesday, November 12, 1952, by Sir John Mann. The building is rather severe but spacious. The sign hanging outside is a punning one, showing on one side a sturdy skipper of the Essex waterways and on the other a large butterfly which would have given Doubleday much joy.

The old town of Harlow is straight down the road from Latton, and its " atmosphere " contrasts strangely with the sterilized, hygienic aura surrounding the new town.

Three inns of varying ages stand in close proximity, the George, the Marquis of Granby and the Chequers. The first has pleasant proportions and a long past. A deed of 1662 exists which was drawn up when the inn was granted for twenty-one years to Francis Poskett, of East Horndon, by Nicholas Sibley: " All that this inn, messuage or tenement with barns, stables, outhouses and buildings, yards and gardens and orchard and a bowling greene thereunto called Great George Inn."

The Chequers too is old, dating back to 1721 at least, and the Marquis of Granby is about the same age. At one time it was called the Wheatsheaf, but changed its name about 1782 to honour the popular hero of the day. Nowadays the Marquis looks somewhat unkempt, but seen through the flowering laburnum growing on its north side the picture it presents is more pleasant.

One other Harlow inn must be mentioned. This is the Green Man, found east of the main road. In coaching days the mail arrived here at four in the morning *en route* to London. Just over twelve hours later the " Telegraph " called on its way to Cambridge from the famed Golden Cross at Charing Cross.

Northwards from Harlow the Cambridge road runs into Hertfordshire. We leave the main road, therefore, to meander northwards by the leafy Essex lanes towards Stane Street. There are no spectacular inns to be found in the small villages. They are unpretentious village inns—just as they should be. They have no exciting story to tell. They have the simplicity and naturalness of the countryside—reflecting the quiet life of the countryman. Through their doors the villager, far removed from the cinema and the lure of big shops, strolls quietly for his pint and a chat with the landlord. Only on Saturday nights is there any semblance of a crowd.

Sheering village is but a short street with the Queen's Head standing centrally among its few houses. In a niche above the doorway is a bust of Queen Victoria—dignified even in her damaged state.

Hatfield Heath is a delight. Houses constructed of varied materials stand around the extensive green, in the centre of which is a cricket pitch. In the summer the White Horse and the Stag are popular grandstands for the thirsty cricket enthusiast.

To the north of Hatfield Heath is Hatfield Forest, once the hunting place of kings but now the property of the nation. Here is to be found the famous Doodle Oak. Not much of the tree is now left, but it is assured of immortality because many writers have introduced it into their works. Perhaps F. Locker Lampson's poem is the best known, particularly the verse:

> " And this was call'd the ' Traitors' Branch '—
> Stern Warwick hung six yeomen stanch
>   Along its mighty fork:
> Uncivil wars for them! The fair
> Red Rose and White still bloom—but where
>   Are Lancaster and York ? "

Where, too, is the Doodle Oak inn? This simpler question can be simply answered—it was closed down in 1955.

QUEENS HEAD

QUEEN'S HEAD ·N·WEALD

CHAPTER XX

DUNMOW TO BRENTWOOD

STANE STREET swings out of Hertfordshire, along through Brewer's End—a village which makes one pause for reflection—through Canfield End and on to Great Dunmow. At the entrance to this famous town is the Queen Victoria, an attractive thatched inn which existed before the queen was born. Of the inns in the main street of Dunmow, the Saracen's Head, with its severe eighteenth-century exterior, is the most imposing. Through the narrow archway we enter the spacious yard, now catering for the modern motor traveller but still boasting coaching stables and harness room.

Entering the inn we find that we have been deceived by the exterior, for the inside is unmistakably Tudor. True, many of the rooms look more Georgian than Tudor, but the older beams continue to peep through! Some rooms contain fine specimens of eighteenth-century furniture, and in the landlord's office is an old whip box.

No one knows when the Saracen's Head started as an inn, but it is recorded that the landlord in the early seventeenth century was the father of Sir Richard Deane, Lord Mayor of London in 1628. Politically he was a supporter of the Roundheads, and Oliver Cromwell himself is said to have stayed in the inn of his supporter.

The Protector would not have approved of a later landlord. As a host he was charming and considerate. Nothing was too much trouble for him. He was a friend, a confidant, and the guests were only too pleased to discuss with him their hopes, their fears, their plans for the future. He encouraged their hopes, placated their fears, and remembered their plans—to such an extent that he grew prosperous. But one night his success came to a sudden end—he was caught in the act of waylaying the coach of one of his recent guests. Then the whole story was revealed—the long series of

robberies of departed guests, his connection with other highwaymen, and his close association with the smugglers of the Essex coast.

Through the lounge windows can be seen the 400-year-old
half-timbered Town Hall with its contemporary clock. It was in
this building that the famous flitch trial was revived about a century
ago. Little Dunmow, and not its greater neighbour, was the place
where the ancient custom originated—a custom so old that even
Chaucer refers to it. The purpose of the trial was to find a man
" which repents him not of his marriage, either sleeping or waking,
in a year and a day." Such a paragon " may lawfully go to Dunmow
and fetch a Gammon of Bacon."

Down the hill from the Town Hall is the Star inn looking up-
wards at the Saracen's Head, its great rival of the coaching era.
From these two inns coaches ran to Bishop's Stortford, Harlow,
Braintree and London.

Farther down the hill is the King's Head. From an unusual seat
recessed in a niche one can look across the road at a pleasant
pond where Lionel Lukin, the designer of one of our first
life-boats, is said to have carried out his experiments. At nearby
Church End the rustic-looking angel on the sign of the Angel
and Harp looks somewhat the worse for drink!

South of Dunmow is a quiet land, a land of small villages joined
by a maze of roads. How difficult it must have been in medieval
times for the pilgrim to find his way northward from Brentwood
to the holy Norfolk shrine where a vial of the virgin's milk was
preserved.

> " Unto the towne of Walsingham
>   The way is hard for you to be gon:
>   And very crooked are those paths
>   For you to find out all alone."

Crooked the paths still are, but the modern pilgrim in search of
rural peace and beauty can do no better than wander round the
Rodings. The first of the villages out of Dunmow, beyond the
inn with the most unusual name of the Kicking Dickey, to bear
the common surname is High Roding. Its inn is the Black Lion,
an old half-timbered structure. Beyond the village narrow lanes
lead eastwards to High Easter. Its two rambling and fully licensed
inns seem extravagant for its small population, but the seeker of
medieval buildings has no room for complaint. The Punch Bowl

has had a recent face-lift and the treatment has improved the comfort. That the Cock and Bell also would benefit from similar treatment is not denied, but the rustic simplicity of the interior would then be lost. No stainless-topped tables here, or leather-covered arm-chairs, but a long deal table scrubbed white, and long benches to match. Their plainness is in keeping with the austere old timber and plain walls. The one polished table must not be overlooked. It is made out of a single elm plank and its surface is marked out for push-ha'penny and other games now long-forgotten. A circular hole has been cut in the adjacent bench and underneath it is a small drawer, a simple arrangement for yet another game—pitch-penny. The players stood at the entrance doorway, about ten feet away, and attempted to throw the coin into the hole, which being but a few inches in diameter demanded a well-paired hand and eye if the thrower was to succeed. I have no doubt that there were, and still are, highly skilled local practitioners of this game, for inn games are played with astonishing enthusiasm and equally marked expertise. The only other example of pitch-penny I know in Essex is to be found in the tap-room of the old Dial House in Bocking.

A couple of miles east of High Easter is one of the best-known villages in the world. Who has not rolled out those lines spoken to John of Gaunt by the Duchess of Gloucester in Shakespeare's Richard II?

> " Bid him,—O, what?
> With all good speed at Plashy visit me.
> Alack, and what shall good old York there see
> But empty lodgings and unfurnish'd walls,
> Unpeopled offices, untrodden stones?"

There was a time when this quiet village of Pleshey resounded to the clank of armour, for here for 250 years resided the Lord High Constable of England. Echoes of the past sometimes fall from the lips of the regulars of the White Horse and the Leather Bottle, but most of the historic allusions are made by the ardent visitors. And what a story it is! Unfortunately, this is no place for it. In the larger inn, the White Horse, hangs a corn dolly made by a local man. There are still a few skilled men practising this art in Essex. The lion and the unicorn in the pavilion of that name in the

Festival of Britain were made of the same material and by Essex men. How long will the craft survive?

This is not the only sadness to cloud our thoughts as we make for Good Easter, for we muse on the slow but sure departure of the young people from the Roding villages, lured by the big towns. Near the centre of the village stands the Star, but the more interesting inn, the Hop Pole, is now a private residence. It stands a short distance out of the village near the two-arched bridge crossing the Canbrook. The name of the inn suggests that hops were grown in the neighbourhood. This is not unlikely, for it is known that there was a hop-ground as late as 1830 near Skreen's Park a couple of miles to the south.

We regain the main road at Leaden Roding. King William IV commands the crossroads. The inn is not very old, so Matthew Levett, the Elizabethan parson of the parish, would not have obtained his ale there. Various accounts of his behaviour hardly suggest a devout man—indeed, quite the opposite! He was notorious as a swearer, a dicer, a carder, a hawker and hunter, a quarreller and a fighter! He was even involved in an unseemly brawl with the parson of Stock in a common inn in Chelmsford on a Christmas Day!

On the road to Fyfield we find what must be the most picturesque off-licence in Essex. Its exact location is difficult to define, for when a local does not know where one Roding begins and another ends what can a stranger say? But really there is no need to pinpoint the building; it is a cottage, newly thatched, standing at right-angles to the road, and cannot be missed.

Fyfield has an inn claiming to be 450 years old. It is the Black Lion, and few will deny its claim.

Around the corner the white-and-black Queen's Head fits in attractively with the dreamy village. The road crosses a pretty stretch of the River Roding, passes the church and winds onwards to Willingale, where the Maltster's Arms stands near one of the smallest telephone exchanges in Essex. At right-angles to the inn is the road to the smaller Bell, which is so much in harmony with the unbelievable rural peace. The air is filled with bird-song, for the great trees around are many and the traffic is infrequent. The Bell looks across the road at two churches sharing the same churchyard! Many stories are invented to explain this unique juxtaposition, but it seems that two rival Norman knights were responsible.

Why they built the parish churches of Willingale Spain and Willingale Doe so near the parish boundary is anybody's guess, but this Norman whimsy has provided an endless topic of conversation for the visitors to the Bell, which stands like a referee overlooking the two rivals.

On the road to Roxwell is the hamlet of Shellow Bowells. I regret that there is no inn in the place. I should have liked to have digressed . . .

Chipping Ongar stands in the heart of acres of quiet country. The busy road that runs through it from Chelmsford to Epping seems an alien element in this vast farmland scattered with villages of musical names and historic associations—Stondon Massey, Doddinghurst, Blackmore, Havering-atte-Bower, Kelvedon Hatch, Navestock, Writtle. This last is a village of some beauty which, however, has no inn to outshine the lovely green, the glistening pond or the wealth of old and interesting houses. The village pond with its ducks and swans forms the base of the great triangle at the apex of which stands the Rose and Crown with its delightful beer garden.

The peace of the village is shattered, particularly at weekends, by the unbecoming haste of the London-bound traffic, which pauses, however, a few miles away in High Ongar, a little village which, nevertheless, seems designed to cope with the invaders, for on the south side of the main road is an adequate pull-in, convenient for the Foresters Arms, the Three Horseshoes and the Red Lion. On the north side a long graveyard lines the road. Hogarth would have made something of the juxtaposition!

Continuing westward towards Epping we arrive at North Weald Bassett and the King's Head, a half-timbered inn of considerable charm both inside and out. The main fireplace is cunningly devised to heat two bar rooms.

Chipping Ongar is an ancient market town, as the very name indicates. It is not as famous as its tiny neighbour, Greensted, with its celebrated church, but is interesting nevertheless. Its inns are not noted for their beauty, indeed on the whole their exteriors are rather drab, but they all lend variety to the diverse architectural styles of the buildings in the High Street. A large signboard standing on the east side of the road proclaims the presence of the King's Head on the opposite side.

It is the largest inn in the town and it has the highest coach entrance, too. The smaller Bell also has a coachway with a room above it. Down the hill, beyond the Royal Oak and the Lion, is—or should I say are?—the Two Brewers. The right fork leads to Greensted church—the vicar of which, incidentally, must be celibate and a teetotaller!

Chipping Ongar's chief coaching inn was the Crown, gone now and largely forgotten. A daily service used to operate between it and the famous Bull in Aldgate.

Frequent mention of the state of the Essex roads has already been made. Those around Ongar were no better. According to the *Kent and Essex Mercury* of November 1825, Ongar roads not only had poor surfaces but were also subject to flooding. In order to warn travellers, however, a workman—was he Irish?—fixed a post in the roadside bearing the notice: " When the water is over this post, it is dangerous to pass."

On the southern outlet of Chipping Ongar the dainty Stag stands on a dangerous corner. The small inn is as cosy inside as it is pretty outside. To the rear is a colourful garden, pleasant to drink in during the summer time. South of the Stag, for several miles the road is lonely and tortuous, with few inns. At Pilgrim's Hatch they become more frequent and one can choose the Black Horse or the neighbouring Rose and Crown, twins in age but not in size. Why is it that black-and-white structures have a never-failing attraction for the Englishman, thirsty or otherwise? Is it beauty alone or does a Tudor house stir the Elizabethan adventurer in us?

We do not know for certain, but one thing we do know—that a young man with that Elizabethan spirit is the landlord of the Rose and Crown (at the time of writing). In 1959 he sailed across the Atlantic single-handed!

The Black Horse has not such a celebrity—how many inns have? —but it has its own charms and attractions. The pleasant lounge opens on to a cool garden from which the fields roll away to Weald Park. The Coach and Horses nearer Brentwood has also a fair garden graced by a weeping willow.

On either side of this Ongar—Brentwood road the quiet countryside is interlaced with a maze of lanes and roads along which it is soothing to wander aimlessly, letting chance lead us to some interesting hostelry. One such inn might be the Green Man at Navestock. Every true son of Essex who has wielded the willow should approach this Mecca with reverence, for was it not here in the year 1790 that the Essex County Cricket Club was formed? So a photostat copy of an original document modestly proclaims in the public bar. From a distance the Green Man looks like a large dwelling house. We are told that originally it was a hunting lodge belonging to Bois Hall in Dudbrook. The inside of the Green Man is even more of a surprise than the outside. The high, airy rooms have the modern look with their contemporary décor and wealth of paintings of exotic women of divers tans by an artist enjoying astonishing popularity at the present time.

What could be more delightful than to enjoy a drink outside the Green Man of a summer's day, lazily watching a game of cricket on the hallowed green, then to retire to an English tea in this self-same inn?

Another inn of sophisticated luxury is the Moat in tiny Dodding-hurst, a village almost lost in the intricate lanes to the east of the Ongar road. The Moat is so unlike its predecessor! Of recent years the brewers have spent a great deal of money rebuilding the older inns and renovating many more both in town and country.

The intentions are excellent, but it can be argued that country pubs require different treatment from town hotels. Frequently the architects seem to have been unaware that the town is different from the country. The pattern of the new establishments both inside and outside is generally of a monotonous similarity. Outside the farmers may be ploughing, the birds singing and a herd of cows returning home to be milked, but inside the patrons can be drinking a gin-and-it or a Tia Maria amid West-end luxury! Surely it is possible to design an attractive and comfortable interior yet still be in harmony with the countryside.

Musings such as these are inevitable to anyone who likes the country. It always comes as a shock to find city sophistication at the end of a country lane. But whatever I might think, I do know that the countless patrons of the Green Man or the Moat would wish me to Jericho. The journey would not be long or unpleasant, for the house of that name is in Blackmore, a small village to the north of Doddinghurst. I shall never forget sitting in the public bar of the Leather Bottle chatting with a local who told me that Henry VIII used to be a frequent visitor to the village. Then I remembered. It was in Jericho House that he installed Elizabeth Talbois and it was there that his natural son Henry Fitzroy was born. When Henry went a-visiting his courtiers discreetly explained that he had gone to Jericho.

Such a chance remark as that heard in the public bar frequently adds to the thrill of the inn searcher. In a moment shorter than it takes to call time one can be sitting in an inn in some quiet village and a casual observation sweeps one's imagination back through the centuries to some great historical event or to some important figure of England's past.

THE BLACK LION
HIGH RODING

CHAPTER XXI

BRAINTREE AND COGGESHALL

WE left Thomas Kemp and his accompanist as he was presenting a pair of garters to Sir Thomas Mildmay. Passing through Chelmsford, the dancer headed north towards Braintree. Today the traveller can proceed quickly along an excellent road so different from the one Kemp encountered. The Romans had left behind a good road joining the two towns when they departed from Essex, but it is unlikely that any repairs or even maintenance were undertaken from the time of their departure till the reign of the first Elizabeth at least. That is the only conclusion we can arrive at when we read Kemp's account of the road to Braintree:

" This foule way I could find no ease in, thicke woods being on eyther side of the lane, the lane likewise being full of deep holes, sometimes I skipt up to the waste. . . . At length, coming to a broad plash of water and mud, which could not be avoyded, I fetcht a rise, yet fell in over the anckles at the further ende. My youth that followed me tooke his jumpe, and stuck fast in the midst, crying out to his companion, ' Come, George, call ye this dancing? Ile go no further,' for indeede he coulde go noe further, till his fellow was fane to wade and helpe him out. I could not chuse but laugh to see howe like to frogges they laboured. . . ."

In Great Leighs is an inn with the unusual sign of St. Anne's Castle. The origin of the name is doubtful, particularly the final word, which is a later addition, for on Ogilby's map of 1765 the inn is simply marked St. Anne's, but by the time Greenwood produced his map in 1824 it was known by its present name. Of course, many explanations have been offered! In White's *Gazetteer of Essex* it is claimed that a hostel stood on the spot " where pilgrims rested to and from the Shrine of St. Thomas à Becket. At the Dissolution it was given to Thomas Jennings, and its site is now occupied by an inn called St. Anne's Castle and said to be the oldest licensed public-house in England." Taylor the Water Poet mentioned it in 1636 when he stated that Will Chandler was a keeper of " innes at Plashie and St. Anne's." In 1955, during some restorations, a fine Tudor window was uncovered. Little has been heard lately about the poltergeist that from time to time caused so much damage inside the inn.

As the inn seeker approaches the heart of Braintree he is delighted to see a fine old inn, the White Hart. Buildings in its neighbourhood have come and gone, but for about 400 years the White Hart has presented more or less the same face to the street. It is mentioned in Bufton's diary under the date April 1682, because in that year, he says, when the justices and a number of other people were meeting in the White Hart the floor collapsed, but the only injury recorded is a broken leg.

The inn has several features of architectural interest in addition to the interesting façade. Many rooms show moulded timbers of Tudor days; the former open galleries that overlooked the court-yard are now walled in; room bells still hang at the coach-yard entrance, while in the archway itself is a stout iron bar which to the modern eye appears to have little purpose but which is really of great interest. In the old pre-fridge days game and meat were suspended from it in the belief that the cool breezes blowing through the archway kept the meat in good condition.

In the archway, too, can be seen a little doorway leading to what was once the room of the night porter, whose presence was so necessary when late travellers sought to gain admission after the great courtyard doors were shut.

Through the archway can be seen a building which, although of little attraction itself, contains some interesting late Georgian features. When it was built about 100 years ago it was one of the most important buildings in Braintree, for in it were held the petty sessions and county court, balls, and most of the other important social gatherings.

Beyond this building is held, every Wednesday, the egg and poultry market, an event which has taken place for many a year—how long nobody knows. Did Bunyan know of it? Maybe, for he was a frequent visitor to Braintree and was often to be heard preaching outside the White Hart and other places in the town.

Another well-known coaching inn was the appropriately named

Horn. It still stands near the centre of the town, but its dignified frontage suggests a later origin than the White Hart.

Like most towns, Braintree had its taverns where the hard-working labourer could forget his week's toil in riotous drinking on Saturday nights. Farm hands from the country round had three such places to choose from, called—with some truth it is said—Little Hell, Great Hell and Damnation. These Bunyan-like names were actually registered as the Three Tuns, the George and the Green Man. It appears that one of the favourite games in these pubs was not darts or shove-ha'penny, but one of strictly local origin. The participants had to spin round on the seat of their pants on the well-sanded floor, the fastest spinner being the winner. This was before the invention of the cocktail shaker—but the result was the same!

To a stranger Braintree is a confusing place. Only a person born and bred locally can distinguish with accuracy the limits of Braintree and Bocking. These towns sit on each other's laps! No doubt if anyone from Bocking happens to read this book he will be infuriated that the White Hart has been assigned to Braintree!

I do not think that anyone will challenge Bocking's claim to the Six Bells, however. It stands on an important corner site, and for about fifty years now " Old Harkilees " has looked down from the position of eminence he occupies on the front of the inn. Does he still descend at midnight and refresh himself—not in the lounge bar as sceptics claim, but in the neighbouring Blackwater?

Where did " Old Harkilees " come from? Where did he get his strange name? About fifty years ago he stood on the ground at the corner of the street, and before that, it is thought, he passed a more domestic existence with his brother—or sister—decorating an Elizabethan fireplace. "Harkilees" is probably an Essex variant of " Hercules," a name not unknown as a Christian name in the district. Two prominent citizens of seventeenth-century Bocking were so called: Hercules Stevens, who built a house in Church Lane in 1600, and Hercules Arthur, who purchased the manor of Fryers in 1632.

Many buildings in Essex are pointed out as old pilgrim hostels. Unfortunately these claims are seldom backed by documentary evidence. Can claims be ignored for that reason? I, for one, do not think so. Let the unbelievers disprove the claim and until then let the rest of us be misguided enough to accept the tradition.

The Six Bells is a case in point. Locally there is a strong belief that the original building, together with some houses adjacent, formed a hostel for pilgrims and wayfarers. The circumstantial evidence is quite strong. The lords of the manor were priors of Christ Church monastery, Canterbury; the hostel stood near an important ford over the Blackwater and near routes which pilgrims would have used heading either southwards for the Thames and Canterbury or northwards for the shrine of Our Lady of Walsingham, or the tomb of St. Edmund at Bury.

Eastwards again to Coggeshall.

Who has not heard of Paycocke's House? It is one of the first houses to be seen as we enter the town, standing next door to the Fleece. This sign is appropriate, for the town's medieval wealth was founded on wool, and the famous house is one of the loveliest examples in Essex of a wool merchant's residence of that period. The cunning hand of the woodcarver enriched the external timbers with running foliage, tiny heads, figures and shields.

But Paycocke's is not the oldest secular building in this town of old buildings. That honour belongs to the Woolpack, a house which Thomas Paycocke would have known well, since it stood so near the church in which he worshipped. The gables have 400-year-old beams and, inside, portions of the trussed roof are even older. However, these ancient parts are but details, and the visitor is more impressed by the warmth and appearance of the interior and the pleasing picture made by the old inn and the church.

From some ancient records we learn that when Thomas Lowrey, vicar of Coggeshall, was ejected from the church in 1665 he purchased the property now known as the Woolpack, although it was not an inn at that time, but when his grandson Jeremiah sold the same property in 1708 to George Long of Coggeshall, a victualler, it was described in the conveyance as a " Common Inn known as the Woolpack and 4 Cottages." These cottages were demolished some time ago and the site is now the Woolpack car park.

The proximity of church and inn has given rise to many a " Coggeshall story." One of these tells of two men who, feeling immensely strong at closing time, decided to move the church. Placing their jackets on the grass, they set to work, but their struggles were unavailing. Perhaps they were pushing against the wind! They decided, therefore, to push from the other side. This time they thought their efforts were more successful and were confirmed in

THE WOOLPACK   COGGESHALL

THE FOX ·FINCHINGFIELD

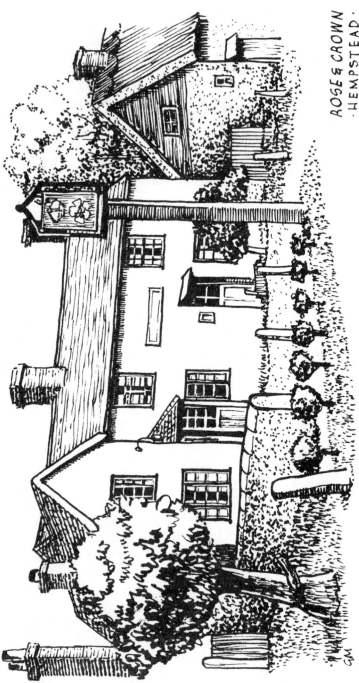

ROSE & CROWN
· HEMPSTEAD ·

this belief when they went to recover their jackets. They were no longer there! Evidently the church had been pushed on top of them!

In the centre of the village is the strangely named Chapel inn. Why Chapel? The solution to the riddle of this strange sign is found in the will of one Thomas Hall, of Cokesale, dated January 15, 1499: " I bequeath towards the edifying and making of a chapell within the said Towne of Cokesale XXS to be paide when the said chapell is in werkying."

The chapel was constructed, for in the " Certificate of Chantry Lands " dated 1549 we read: " Item, an olde chaple in the street there [Coggeshall], with a little Garden, which is worth by the year 4s."

In 1588, a messuage called the Old Chapel was conveyed to the fullers and weavers of Coggeshall. The building was demolished in 1795. Chapel inn occupies a part of the site and perpetuates the name.

Gangsters is not a word generally used in the same context as peaceful Coggeshall, but for the five years from 1844 the " Coggeshall gang " terrorized the village and neighbourhood. Their headquarters was the Black Horse. The gangsters were extremely ruthless to their victims; old and young alike were ill-treated by these masked bandits, who were armed with pistols and cudgels. A remarkable aspect of their raids, which always took place in the dead of night, was the fact that food as well as money was stolen and frequently consumed on the burgled premises.

The reign of terror lasted five years, because the police were already fully occupied trying to stamp out the widespread incendiarism—a result of the bitterness found among the many unemployed farm labourers of the district. Eventually one of the Coggeshall gang was caught, but it still proved difficult to apprehend the others, since they immediately dispersed and headed for the ports in an attempt to leave the country. Eventually they were all arrested and tried, the leader being transported for life and the others for periods ranging from seven to fifteen years.

FLITCH of BACON
LITTLE DUNMOW

CHAPTER XXII

THROUGH THE HOP-LANDS

ETWEEN Stane Street and the northern boundary of Essex
are wide areas that have undergone little change through
the centuries. This is a region of villages—even the towns
are just big villages—and consequently, with few exceptions, the
inns are village inns and the regular customer is the slow-changing
Essex countryman. It is in these inns that you hear the authentic
accent of Essex, a slow drawl laced with delightful dialect words
redolent of the field and of village life.

Of the many lovely villages of this quiet land, perhaps the most
famous is Finchingfield. Anyone who has dipped into a picture-
book proclaiming the beauties of England will already be acquainted
with this most photographed of villages. Houses of varying architectural styles stand round the rim of a saucerlike depression which
holds the green and the village pond. On one occasion I was enjoying
the scene in the company of two Swedes on their first visit to
England. Their delight was unbounded. " Just like a caricature of
what we expected England to be" was their verdict, and a more apt
description would be difficult to coin. Stand in front of the Fox—
the pargeted inn on the east side of the green—feasting your eyes
on the surrounding loveliness, and you enjoy the very essence of
what is best in Essex.

No one would claim that Great Bardfield could rival Finchingfield for beauty, but it is a delightful village nevertheless, and this
opinion is shared by the small band of distinguished artists who
have made their homes here. You might meet them at odd times
in the Bell, the Vine or the half-timbered White Hart, which displays
the date 1629 on a gable. The Bell sports an actual bell for its sign
while graceful ironwork cunningly wrought into vine leaves and
tendrils supports the sign-board of its neighbour.

East of Finchingfield and Great Bardfield we enter the former

hop country. In 1767 Arthur Young wrote: " Around Henning-
ham . . . hops are much cultivated. More than 200 acres grow
near the town, and let on medium at about £3 an acre, unless hired
with a farm, in which case they are lett cheaper."

The Hedinghams seem to have been the centre of the cultivation.
Certain it is that hops were grown in Castle Hedingham for three
centuries, persisting long after they had vanished from other parts
of Essex, to die out at last in 1887.

Systematic hop culture was introduced into north Essex some
time during the first quarter of the sixteenth century.

> " Hops, Reformation, Bays and Beer,
>   Came into England all in a year."

As Norden wrote in 1607, the " lowe and springie grounde "
proved most suitable and the cultivation became widespread. The
same writer had stated in 1594 that the hundreds of Lexden, Fresh-
well, Kinckford and Dunmow " abounde greatlie with hopps, a
commoditie of greate and continuall use, but draweth with it an
inconvenience—the destruction of young springes."

To provide the poles for supporting the hops, spinneys of ash
and spanish chestnut were planted in Finchingfield and Castle
Hedingham to meet the very heavy demand. Indeed, so great was
it that many an Essex woodland completely disappeared as a result.

I have written a great deal about beer and ale—indeed, without
these there would be no inns and no book, and the first we would all
deplore!—so a word about the part played by hops in the manufacture of these drinks would not be amiss.

The native English ale up to the mid-sixteenth century was
flavoured with wormwood, ground-ivy or even a roasted crab
apple called a " toast "—as we note in Bishop Still's rollicking song:

> " I love no roast but a nut brown toast,
>   And a crab laid in the fire;
> A little bread shall do me stead,
>   Much bread I do not desire."

The hop flavour was probably introduced by the Dutch and
Flemish weavers in the time of Edward III. We know that there
were at least six " hop-planters " in Colchester in 1571. The crop
was profitable, so much so that the tendency was to abandon
arable farming to devote a greater acreage to hops. Men and money

being the same then as now, the state found it necessary to restrict the area devoted to hop cultivation—a law which applies even to this day.

Hops flavour the beer. Malt is the basic ingredient of the beverage, and in this country at the present time this is obtained from barley. The barley grain—which has to be nursed most carefully—stores its vital energy in the form of starch. In natural germination this starch is converted into sugar, a product easily assimilable by the tender plant. This process continues until such time as the plant can manufacture its own food by the normal photosynthetic process.

In the maltings the conversion of the starch to sugar is induced artificially, but the process is stopped at the moment when the embryo plant is about to absorb the sugar to give it a start in life. This thieving process is known as malting.

This is done in practice by steeping the grains for some fifty-four hours until about forty per cent water is absorbed. These well-soaked grains are then spread on a cement floor and in eight days about half a dozen rootlets appear on each grain, indicating that the protective cellular wall around the starch has broken down. The barley is now known as green malt. To prevent the plant from growing and thus using up the sugar, the barley is transferred to a kiln, where the malt is heated to kill the enzyme " cystase " and make dormant the enzyme " diastase."

Water is added to the malt and the mixture allowed to fall into a " mash tun," where after standing for a certain length of time, at a certain temperature, the diastatic action breaks down the starch into sugars and the resultant liquid, called " wort," is drained off into large coppers.

It is at this stage that hops are added. They not only impart flavour to the wort but also help to act as a preservative. Thomas Tusser, the Essex farmer-turned-poet, has expressed the facts in verse in his *Five Hundred Points of Good Husbandrie:*

> " The hop for his profit I thus do exalt,
>   It strengtheneth drink, and it flavoureth malt;
>   And being well brewed, long kept it will last,
>   And drawing abide—if you draw not too fast."

After the hops are added, the mixture is boiled for approximately two hours, at which point the hopped wort is strained and passed through a cooling plant to the fermenting vessels. Yeast is added and the fermentation commences. Carbon dioxide is released and alcohol produced. The yeast thrives, reproduces itself and forms a scum on top of the liquid, but most of it is skimmed off. About five days later the resultant liquid is what we have been waiting for—beer!

It will not be ready for drinking, though, until a few days later, if you favour mild beer. Present-day stronger beers require maturing for three months or more before they are fit for the palate.

The Hedinghams have changed but little since their hop-growing days. Castle Hedingham still looks like a feudal village, its houses huddling round the walls of the great keep erected by the mighty Earls of Oxford, some of whose devices are still used as inn signs throughout Essex—the star and the boar's head, for example. These and other badges can be seen above the west window of the village church.

The Bell is, without doubt, the most important of the village inns, although now but a shade of its former self. You would hardly think that meetings held in the long room of this village inn were important enough to have been featured in the leaders of *The Times*, but such was the case. Every year the Hinckford Hundred Conservative Club used to meet here to be addressed by a distinguished representative of the Tories. Even Disraeli descended to this quiet spot to inebriate the listeners with his verbosity!

In those days the Bell was an important stage. The old Bury coach stopped here on its way from the Angel, Bury St. Edmunds, to the Green Dragon, Bishopsgate Street. But the Bell was another victim of the railways. For a few years it tried to compete, but in 1847 it acknowledged its defeat and abandoned the struggle.

In the churchyard is a memorial to the dead of World War I. It consists of the shaft and base of a twelfth-century cross which were found in the cellars of the Falcon.

Out of this medieval world peopled by the ghosts of mighty knights we wander down the Colne to Halstead. Even when we reach this hilly town we are not free of the haunting past, for was it not here that John Bourchier, second Baron Berners, lived—the man who translated Froissart's *Chronicles*, that incomparable tapestry of the Middle Ages?

In the church of St. Andrew are the fine tombs of this family, but our interest in the church lies in other directions—in the gotch housed there. It is one of four to be found in Essex. The others are in Colchester Museum and in the church in Hornchurch (two), but they are not as big as the Halstead example. This four-and-a-half-gallon ringers' jug, or gotch, seems to have been an essential part of the bellringers' equipment in days gone by. Anyone who has witnessed the great expenditure of energy when a Bob Major is rung can easily understand why! In fairness to the Halstead ringers it should be made clear that this gotch was used chiefly in the festive season. What the Puritans thought of its use even on such occasions we do not know, and we mention this because the jug was actually made in their day—in 1658 to be exact. On New Year's Eve the gotch was carried round the village, and liquid donations were poured into it. The brim-full vessel was then carried back to the belfry and placed on a block in the centre, so that thirsty ringers could fill their tankards with the " hot pot " (as this rough-and-ready cocktail was called) from the spigot at the bottom.

Inscribed on the pot in capitals are the date and the initials of the ringers of that time as well as the following doggerel verses:

23 AUGUST 1658

SD IH GT	RH IM
IM. BE MERRY AND WISE	IN SUMMER HEATE
USE ME MUCH AND BREAK ME NOT	AND WINTER COLD
FOR I AM BUT AN EARTHEN POT	TO DRINK OF THIS
	WE DARE BE BOLD

AS WE SIT BY THE FYRE TO KEEPE OURSELVES WARME
THIS POT OF GOOD LIQUOR WILL DOE US NO HARME

IF YOU BE WICE
FIL ME NOT TWICE
AT ONE SITTING

Even one filling should have been enough to account for some strange " changes." No records are extant of the New Year ringings—which is a pity!

There is no potter's mark or place of origin on the pot, but it is not unlikely that it was made at Gestingthorpe, for that pottery was active from the early seventeenth century to 1913.

Pevsner remarks: " The town of Halstead is not one of the most attractive of Essex. There are things only here and there which need picking out." We pick out the Bull, standing in the shade of the great chestnuts at the foot of the town hill. Do not be misled by the frontage, for most of the building behind this late façade dates from the sixteenth century, including the massive chestnut beams and the pegged roof timbers. One of the beams in the saloon bar has been burnt hollow and was used as a " safe " by a former landlord. The fireplace in the same bar was discovered about twenty-five years ago when a small fireplace was removed. It has two chimneys and a wooden " salt " shelf. In the dining room the central oven is of unusual design, containing two smaller ovens used at one time for baking bread. A lounge door is of the old Essex latch variety. The present landlord informed me that it is believed that Dickens once stayed in the Bull, and added, " At least this is a change from Queen Elizabeth ! "

We wander north from Halstead church to a less-famed one at Birdbrook. In the tower of this village church is a tablet to one Martha Blewitt, who died in the Swan in 1861. The good lady had a remarkable marital record: she married nine husbands—one after the other, of course! For the funeral sermon the parson chose as his text: " Last of all ye woman dy'd allsoe." In the following century a Robert Hogan of the same village married seven wives, but it is not known if he was trying to break Martha's record. Was it the good air of the district or the good beer of the Swan which accounted for such endurance?

It is difficult to imagine a more pleasant occupation than wandering around these lanes of north Essex, arriving unexpectedly at delightful villages with equally delightful inns, taking a drink with the landlord, and discussing the weather, the crops or some everyday topic. Strangely enough, these perennial subjects do not seem out of place in such surroundings, for these village inns and their landlords are close to the soil—and this is not meant as adverse criticism. Seldom has anything noteworthy happened in them or to them. The Rose and Crown, Hempstead, is an exception. Such a peaceful picture is difficult to associate with that far from peaceful character Dick Turpin, but an oil painting near the front door and various relics inside the inn help to remind us that Turpin was born in this inn. A copy of the church register records his birth in the year 1705, various prints in the bar parlour picture his exploits and a delightful piece of Rockingham china represents the rogue in 3-D. And I must not forget the spyhole! This is in the ceiling beam near the wall and is said to have been used by Dick.

Opposite the inn is a group of trees known as " Turpin's Ring," and a number of legends have been foisted on it. Black Bess was tied up there when Turpin was visiting his parents. At a later date rumour has it that cockfights were held in it.

Westward of Hempstead the lanes wander in all directions through the pleasant countryside, but it is possible by friendly questioning to find Saffron Walden!

To arrive at that sweet-named town is an event. You feel that there should be a fanfare of post-horns as you arrive at the top of the hill to sweep down the tree-lined street, past the sixteenth-century Greyhound, to pull up at the Crosskeys standing at the bottom of the dip. The front of this building faces the High Street and seems to have been part of the original inn. The long extension in King Street consisted in the late fifteenth century of two buildings, one part being a shop. The corner post of the Crosskeys is said to have been a living tree.

The appearance of the inn clearly indicates its Tudor origin, while that of the Rose and Crown suggests the Georgian period. In the latter case, however, appearances prove to be deceptive, for this inn was serving ale a quarter of a century before Shakespeare was born! One Eden Nesfield was responsible for designing the present façade in 1874—a pleasing symmetry of rectangles arranged around a shell porch. This was not the first time for the old inn to have a " face lift ": " This house was fronted with brick in 1690, by William Patch, owner and keeper of the same, and the same was new sashed and beautified in the year 1749." This information was discovered on a manuscript when the inn was undergoing internal alterations in 1916. So what Nesfield really did was to restore and embellish this early alteration.

Shakespeare was mentioned above and there is good reason to believe that he stayed at the Rose and Crown. His company did visit the town in 1607 and gave a performance in the inn, so it is assumed that the playwright himself sojourned there. There is also another tradition—that the mysterious W.H. was no other than the landlord of the inn at the time, William Holgate.

A few doors away lived Gabriel Harvey, a poet who was friendly with Spenser and patronized by Leicester. He appeared, too, in several other poems of a much less complimentary nature, which is not surprising, for he was an extremely quarrelsome person. Greene, in his *A Quip for an Upstart*, alluded to his origin as the son of a ropemaker, but perhaps the best known reply to Harvey was the poem by Nash entitled " Have with you to Saffron Walden, or Gabriell Harveys Hunt is up."

Another Walden poet was Robert Winstanley, who in 1678 wrote his *Perambulations from London to Saffron Walden*. In it we find:

> " I'll show you whence my journey I did trace,
> It was from the Rose and Crown where Mr. Eve
> Doth keep a house like to an Under Sherriff;
> There is good Sack, good French wine, and good beer."

No doubt this landlord was the one whose name appears in the manor book from time to time. For instance, in 1680 when Charles II paid a visit to Audley End we read that the corporation " Pd. Mr. Eve for wine at the Dinner Ec., when the King came to Audley End, when we delivered the Address................£5. 2. 0d."

A less happy occasion also required wine.

> " 1654. Payd 2 men that pursued Moulton when
> he broke out of gaol ..   ..   1s. 4d.
> Payd for fetters for Moulton & Douglas   .. 16s.
> For one quart of canary at the Rose, when
> Moulton & Douglas suffered   ..   ..   2s.
> Knocking off their rivets   ..   ..   ..   1s. 6d."

What crime they suffered for we are not told.

But the festive occasion which I find most entertaining took place in 1814, when two oxen had to be roasted to cater for the many guests. The celebration was " to enable the poor to partake of the general joy of their country and of Europe, upon the glorious occasion of the return to peace."

There was no excuse for " the poor " to behave in an unseemly manner. The instructions were explicit: " Each person and family to come neatly dressed, and to bring small mugs and glasses, knives, forks, etc., for their own use, and to take their plates, knives and forks into their baskets as soon as dinner is over and to send them home."

When the bugle was sounded everybody was to be silent for grace to be pronounced. The beer was served by " industrious mechanics," but the " yeomen and gentry, by their kind and Christian condescension " carved the oxen.

We are not informed how many Christian yeomen and gentlemen

were present, but they must have worked hard to provide for the 2,600 persons who sat down at the seventy-five tables.

Games followed the meal and, later in the evening, the festivities ended in a firework display. The town had to foot the bill of £32/12/11.

No comparable celebration has taken place since that memorable occasion; but if you are in Saffron Walden on the Saturday before mid-Lent, go through the yard of the Rose and Crown to the extensive common, the green of which is splashed with the gaudy yellows, reds and blues of a lively fair, and where the birdsong is drowned by the raucous songs of yesteryear.

On the way through the inn yard note the simple pargeting. The efforts which bedeck the front are more ambitious—roses, crowns and bunches of grapes. But to see pargeting at its most elaborate a visit to the Sun inn is called for. It is no longer an inn although it is still known by that appellation.

This famous building in Church Street was built some time in the fifteenth century. The plaster work on the front was applied 200 years later and consists chiefly of a huge sun and representations of Thomas Hickathrift and the Wisbech giant.

Inside the house a tile was found decorated with a portrait of Oliver Cromwell. This simple tile, now in the local museum, recalls a meeting of historical importance—that between Cromwell and the Commissioners of Parliament. It was held at a time when there was trouble with the Army and, as Carlyle wrote: " We can conceive a universal sorrow and anger, and all manner of dim schemes and consultations going on at Saffron Walden."

Although Cromwell received the thanks of Parliament for the apparent settlement, the discontent continued. Carlyle quoted three letters written by Cromwell in Saffron Walden dated May 1647. And it is not unlikely that it was in the Sun that Cromwell and his officers resolved to seize Charles.

Long after the Protector died his sobering influence was still felt. In 1775, for instance, there is a quarter sessions minute which " ordered that Innkeepers . . . within this town do keep good order within their respective houses . . . and that they do not suffer any person to continue Drinking or Tippling therein during the time of Divine Service on the Lord's day . . . and shall entertain no strollers, amblers or persons travelling with Sights, Faires or other entertainments of the Stage, nor suffer any playing at

Cards, Bowls, Loggotts, Coytes, or other Games, Cockfighting, Drunkenness or Disorders wt. soever."

Half-way between Saffron Walden and Great Dunmow lies Thaxted. It is a quiet town with buildings that have mellowed into a pleasing harmony. The magnificent church tends to overpower the many interesting buildings to be found throughout the town. It is difficult to realize that this village was an important centre for the manufacture of wool and cutlery in the Middle Ages. Thaxted as a miniature Sheffield seems somewhat incongruous to the present-day visitor!

Opposite the church stands the Swan with its pleasant late-Georgian front concealing an older structure dating back to the days of Henry VIII. It is recorded that in 1548 Walter Spylman died *ad segnum Scygni*. He had acquired the property nine years earlier. Beneath the inn yard are large cellars of indeterminate age. The oast house and maltings which stood in the yard have long since disappeared.

Did the workmen who built the church obtain their ale across the road in the Swan or from the ancient Cock inn? There is a strong tradition that the latter was the favoured hostelry. Outside the inn are seats, a delightful amenity, for even to look on the church bathed in the warm glow of a summer evening is inspiring.

From Thaxted a pleasant road runs northwards through quiet country to meet the important London—Newmarket road at Newport. There the peace of the countryside gives way to the noise of the arterial road which slices the village in half and does not encourage the traveller to stay and contemplate the many architectural attractions of the place. Fortunately, one of the most interesting buildings, the Crown House, stands on a loop off the main highway. In the time of Charles II it was an inn, it is believed, called the Horn. The monarch is said to have been a regular visitor to the place, for it housed no other than Nell Gwynne. The truth of this claim is not proved, but it is not unlikely that Charles did visit the inn, Nell or no Nell, on his way to Newmarket or to Audley End, a palace which he acquired but did not pay for.

Crown House was built towards the end of the sixteenth century, but the delightful shell porch was added about 100 years later, when the whole front was also decorated with pargeting.

Another inn patronized by travellers to Newmarket still adorns the main road with its picturesque half-timbering. This is the

Coach and Horses, where both Villiers, second Duke of Buckingham, and the Earl of Rochester are said to have stayed frequently.

To the north, near the bridge over the junior Granta, stands the old toll house, still retaining its board of toll charges.

" Tolls payable at this Gate	d.
For every Waggon, Van or Cart	2
For every Horse, Mare, Gelding or Mule, led or driven (not drawing or rode)	1
For every Ass led or driven (not drawing or rode)	½
For every drove of Oxen, Cows or neat Cattle per Score	4
For every Ox, Cow or herd of neat Cattle less than a Score	1
For sheep and pigs per score	½
For every sheep or pig less than a score ..	½
For every Bull	4

Parishes exempt from the payment of Tolls.

Newport, Wicken, Saffron Walden, Great Chesterford, Little Chesterford, Wendens, Quendon and Widdington."

Northwards from Newport the road runs to the Essex boundary, where it forks, one branch going to Cambridge, the other to Newmarket. The improvement in the latter in the seventeenth century was almost certainly due to the desire of Charles II to speed his journey to his palace at Newmarket. Later the road became a great coaching highway and important inns sprang up along it.

We stop short of the border at the unpretentious Greyhound in Great Chesterford to reflect on all we have seen and heard in our wanderings around the inns of Essex and to wonder how much still remains undiscovered. There is not a village without its inn, and no inn without its story. The lode of lore is rich but buried deep, and the task of the prospectors is one of some difficulty because the records are few and frequently hidden beneath such an accumulation of hearsay and vagueness that the location proves long and laborious. But the search is worth while, for the rewards are varied and rich.

CROSS KEYS · SAFFRON WALDEN

THE RABBITS · STAPLEFORD ABBOTS

CHAPTER XXIII

INN SIGNS OF ESSEX

ALTHOUGH the signs dealt with in this chapter are restricted to the inns mentioned in the book, there are sufficient examples to illustrate the general principles underlying inn nomenclature.

Inn signs, barbers' poles and the three brass balls of the pawn-broker are almost the only trade signs left us of the multiplicity that formerly existed. Distinctive signs were necessary at a time when the population was largely illiterate, but the extremes to which some shopkeepers went to advertise their calling necessitated legislation as early as the fifteenth century, because it was said that the great size and number of signs in the streets of London prevented the access of sunlight and the free circulation of air. The nuisance was abated for a while, but in the reign of Charles II we again find an order to the effect " that in all streets no sign-board shall hang across, but that the sign shall be fixed against the balconies, or some convenient part of the house." A century later yet another order was issued, and if we look at Tyland's drawing of Chelmsford in 1762 we understand why. The swinging sign of the Black Boy hangs from a beam extending from the house to a support about thirty feet away. In the foreground of the drawing is another sign, presumably of the Lion inn, which must be about forty-five feet high. It was not the height, however, but the position which must have been troublesome to the town's traffic, since the sign stands right in the middle of the road!

Before the signs ran wild a simple bush hanging from a pole was sufficient to indicate an alehouse. Indeed, prior to the passing of the first licensing Act in the reign of Edward VI the placing of such a bush outside was all that was necessary if a person wished to sell ale. Certain reasonable conditions were imposed as to purity, price and measure, and in Saxon times infringement of these rules might land the brewer on the ducking stool.

In some earlier chapters it has been suggested that some of the first hostels were attached to monastic establishments and others to the manor house. Absentee landlords, including the king, found that the letting of their mansions when they were not in residence was most profitable. Their arms, or part of their arms, displayed in some prominent position on the building, were precursors of the inn signs. And what splendid signs they make, even to this day!

Crown manors, since they usually occupied favourable positions on the highways, were among the earliest houses used for dispensing hospitality to the wayfarer, and it is a fact that some of our oldest inns bear the crown for a sign. Not that all Crown inns were once crown manors, since the sign was sometimes adopted because the house was built on crown land, or simply because the landlord was patriotic.

The monarchy and the arms and badges of monarchy have always been popular subjects for signboards. King's Heads and Queen's Arms abound. After the Restoration the prevalence of these signs was noticed by the wits who claimed " the King's Head might be empty but the King's Arms were always full." The head shown on these signs is not that of Charles I as one would expect, but that of Henry VIII. King William the Fourth overlooks the crossroads at Leaden Roding, probably because the inn was licensed in his reign. The Rose and Crown dates from the seventeenth century, when the conflict between the red and white roses, between the houses of York and Lancaster, was finally resolved. Lions—red, white and black—are numerous. The red variety is the lion of Scotland. It was also the badge of John of Gaunt. On the arms of the Dukes of Norfolk is a white lion, and on the de Crespignys' a black one.

Understandably, Kentish inns display the white horse more frequently than do those of Essex, since it is the county emblem. The white hart, however, is popular in both counties. Richard II adopted the badge when he ascended the throne and at a tournament held in 1390 the king's men had tabards, shields and horse-covering " browdyd all with whyte hertys." Shakespeare remarks that Jack Cade's headquarters were at the White Hart, Southwark. The great number of White Harts is puzzling, but the reason might be traced to the fourteenth century, when the growth of a new class of manufacturers coincided with the breakdown of the feudal system. Accommodation was proving inadequate for the new rich, so inns were erected to cater for them. Since these new buildings were independent of monastery and manor, they had to look around for a distinctive sign. Why not the badge stamped on their new licence and worn by the king's officers?

The spread eagle was a badge of Henry IV, as was also the swan. The latter bird was also a favourite of Henry V and of the de Bohuns. In Essex, however, it is likely that the Swan inns bear the badge of the de Mandevilles, one-time Earls of Essex. Edward IV used a black bull as a badge and as a sinister supporter to his arms. The third Edward favoured the sun, as did many another monarch, but it must not be overlooked that it was also a charge in the arms of the Distillers' Company.

In the church at Castle Hedingham the badges of the powerful de Veres lend colour to the interior. These same badges can be seen on many an Essex inn, the blue boar and the star being the most common. In the battle of Barnet in 1471 this star (" mullet argent," as the heralds say) displayed on shields of the followers of the Earl of Oxford led to the defeat of the Lancastrians. The morning was misty and the Earl of Warwick, mistaking the silver mullet for the sun in splendour, the badge of the Yorkists, wrongly commanded that his allies be attacked! Suspecting treachery, the de Vere men fled the field and the Lancastrians were defeated.

Outside the Whitmore Arms in Orsett swing the colourful arms of the Lord Lieutenant of Essex and the family crests stand in bold relief on many a house in the village. Great Warley's Headley Arms has been noted. This, like the Wake Arms in Epping Forest, is named after a noted family.

Arms of many companies, some of ancient origin, have been appropriated for inn signs. The black boy, or to be more exact a demi-Moor, was the crest of the Tobacco-pipe Makers' Company, which was incorporated as long ago as 1663. For supporters the company used two young Moors proper. Many families, too, used a black man's head as their crest, but frequently the connection between the sign and these arms cannot be traced. It is more than likely that there was no connection.

The Three Cups are derived from the Salters' Company, and the Three Tuns either from the arms of the Brewers' Company or from those of the Vintners' Company. Salt was of great importance in the Middle Ages, consequently the company, incorporated in 1327, was one of the richest in London. Covered cups also appear on the arms of the Goldsmiths' Company. Pepys, it may be recalled, visited the old Three Tuns at Charing Cross, where Mr. Throgmorton treated him to wine and bribed him with " five pieces of gold."

When a group of three objects appears on a sign the origin is certain to be heraldic, even though it is not always possible to indicate the exact origin. The Three Crowns is a good example. The Drapers' Company and the Skinners' Company both used three crowns as charges on their shields, as did the Essex family of Wiseman. But the sign is found even on the Continent, so the arms quoted are unlikely to explain the wider use. Now the three crowns represent the three kings, those magi who bore the gold, frankincense and myrrh to the holy stable. St. Helen, it is claimed, discovered the remains of the wise men and placed them in the cathedral of Cologne. Do not the arms of Cologne bear three crowns to honour the event? Cologne was famed, too, for its linen and thread; the best quality was marked with the three crowns.

In Marks Tey is the Trowel and Hammer, a workmanlike sign deriving from the arms of the Plasterers' Company.

Lastly there are those fictitious arms that originated in the heads of befuddled landlords. The one example in this book will suffice as an illustration—the Freemasons' Arms.

Great popular figures or events, historic or otherwise, that caught the imagination of the nation feature prominently as inn signs. The George sign is common, displaying either the features of a king or an action study of England's patron saint. The King's Head is not that of Charles I as is generally supposed but usually that of Henry VIII, but other kings from our island story are not neglected. Sheering has a Queen's Head and displays a bust of Queen Victoria. A widespread favourite is the Royal Oak, the tree in question being the Boscobel oak used by Charles as a hiding place after his defeat at Worcester. Another historic tree gave its name to the King's Oak in Epping Forest. Henry VIII, it is said, waited beneath its shade to hear the sound of those guns which would signal the death of Anne Boleyn. Newport's Crown House (an inn no longer) is the place where Nell awaited her Charles. The Capital or Grand of Southend became the Royal Hotel after the Princess of Wales (later Queen Caroline) had spent a short holiday in the adjoining terrace.

Marlborough appears in Rochford, Nelson in Harwich; but

Admiral Rous is found inland on Galleywood Common. He is not out of place though, for was not he the father of English racing? In Colchester is the Marquis of Granby, still as bald-headed as ever he was.

Inn signs are a kind of shorthand to the history and geography of a county. They give a fair summary of the major activities. Essex, being mainly agricultural, would be expected to display harrows, wheatsheaves, bulls and sheepcotes. It does. The frequency of Ship inns, far removed from the coast as Noah's ark on Ararat, suggest that they should be Sheep inns—the transformation being due to Essex pronunciation. The Forest of Essex, once covering so much of the county, is now represented by that fragment called Epping Forest, but the denizens of the deep woods, the roebuck, the bald-faced stag and the plain stag, decorate many an inn outside the present forest boundaries. In Ingatestone, the Chase stands at the junction of three Essex hunts, but the Fox is away in Finchingfield. In North Stifford the dog pairs up with a partridge, but in East Mersea the pheasant is its companion. Medieval hunting is represented by the Falcon of Wivenhoe and the one still hovering near the seat of the mighty Earls of Oxford at Castle Hedingham. More homely coursing is not forgotten. Saffron Walden has a Greyhound and a Spotted Dog. And the Gun in Dedham must surely be of the hunting sort, for the people of Suffolk are peaceful enough.

Many of the birds and animals found on inn signs are strangers to the Essex fields, woods or air. Their violent heraldic colours would be poor camouflage indeed—but do provide us with a clue as to their origin. Cockfighting is remembered in the numerous Cocks, but the Hawk does not always recall hawking, for both Edward III and Richard II used the falcon as one of their badges. It was also part of the arms of the Stationers' Company. The Swan has already been noted and is more easily explained than the former Cock and Pie of Stanford-le-Hope! Two explanations are offered. One is that the landlord of a Cock inn became landlord of the Magpie and, as so often happened, impaled the signs, which were later shortened to the Cock and Pie. (It would not be out of place here to recall that the daughter of a Cock inn in this area married the son of the Bull inn!) The other derivation suggests that the original sign was Peacock Pie, a popular dish at one time. When this dish went out of fashion, and later out of mind, the sign was shortened to Cock and Pie. Even this became incomprehensible and was later changed to the Cock and Magpie.

The Three Rabbits suggests an heraldic origin, as does the Black Bull. The latter was one of the badges of Edward IV. He also used it for a sinister supporter. Bull inns do not always derive from the animal however. Frequently the source is the papal *bulla* or bull. Snakes seldom appear on inn signs, for obvious reasons. We have a unique example in Essex, however, in the Viper at Fryerning.

One of the newest signs in the county is to be found in Harlow. It has just emerged from a chrysalis as it were, and has been aptly christened the Essex Skipper.

That Essex is closely connected with the sea is amply borne out by its inn signs. Our Jolly Sailor can board the Ship, a New Ship in preference to an Old Ship or even the Old Victory of Nelson, moored alongside the Wharf, weigh Anchor, then, with its Essex Skipper, plough through the Wave to plant the British Flag in the far corners of the Globe.

On the other hand, the Jolly Sailor might not be so adventurous. In that case his craft would be a Thames Barge, a Lobster Smack or a Peter Boat plying their trade within reasonable distance of the Waterman's Arms and always feeling secure in the presence of the Lifeboat.

County crafts and trades, ancient and modern, have not been neglected. Thatchers, bricklayers and brewers are all represented either by a " proper " painting or by an appropriate symbol from their respective arms. The Fleece and the Woolpack remind us of the importance of wool in the medieval economy. Is the fleece the golden one of Jason or the one used as a pendant by the celebrated order? It was in 1430 that Philip, Duke of Burgundy and Count of Flanders, founded the order " to perpetuate the memory of his great revenues raised by wools with the Low Countries." Larwood and Hotten were cynical about this sign. They suggested that " a fleece at the door of an inn or public house looks like a warning of the fate a traveller may expect within."

" Gules, a woolpack argent " were the arms of the London Company of Woolmen, founded about 1300. When the law lords sat down in the Upper House they were ever reminded of one of the main sources of the country's wealth because their comfortable seats were woolpacks. They now have a modern substitute, but the seat of the Lord Chancellor is still known as the Woolsack.

Miscellaneous signs

Some of the most interesting signs cannot be placed in any particular category. Bells of varying numbers are extremely common. Proximity to the church might account for some, but where the bells are numerous hand-bell ringing is suggested as the source. In High Easter is the unusual Cock and Bell sign. When the cock is alone, cockfighting or that very cruel Shrovetide sport the throwing of stones at cocks mounted on stools, but the cock combined with the bell suggests another origin. At one time the schoolmaster held the monopoly of providing game birds for his pupils. The one who owned the winning bird was allowed to wear a bell in his cap for the next three Sundays.

Other miscellaneous signs are also open to various interpretations. The unusual Goat and Boot has been explained in two ways; as a corruption of the Dutch *Der Goden Boode* (the Gods' Messenger) or for the phrase " goat in boots," which Miller Christy regards as caricature of a Welshman.

Another compound name is the Ship and Shovel. The Shovel seems to be a reference to Sir Clowdisley Shovel, Admiral of the Fleet during the reign of William and Mary. As we noted earlier, some of these impaled signs occurred when a new landlord combined the sign of his former house with that of the new. The Sun and Whalebone at Latton seems to be of this kind. Essex has its fair share of whalebones. Were they obtained from whales stranded on the banks of the Thames? Many unusual creatures suffered that fate, but some authorities query this theory and suggest that the bones were obtained from Greenland whalers.

St. Anne's Castle, Chapel Inn, Halfway House, the Chequers and the World's End have already been explained in the appropriate places. A few others complete this section. At Witham the " Young Lady," you may recall, praised the Blue Posts. Perhaps, instead of a sign, the inn was known by the colour of its door-posts. In High Easter the Punch Bowl reminds us of the potent drink. An old Essex recipe, guaranteed efficacious against the rheumy airs of the flats or the biting easterlies, was concocted of the following ingredients: " Take five quarts of brandy, eight quarts of water, and two of new milke; four dozen lemons, three nutmegs, a pound and a halfe of double refined sugar; pare one dozen of the lemons very thin, leaving none of the white, infuse the parings in some of the brandy about three hours with the nutmegs grated, dissolve the sugar in water before you putt it into the brandy, squeeze in the lemons and let all the ingredients be mixed together, then put them all into a bag of thick flannel and let it run without stirring, let about a quart run out, then put it into the bag againe, and so repeate it till it is fine."

Take a long drink of the milk punch and you will believe any of the theories that have been put forward to explain the Crooked Billet sign! A billet is a log of wood, and is so represented on most signs. One writer suggests that just as a bush was hung up as a beer house sign it was but a short step to a crooked stick. This explanation seems too simple.

Fortunately there is no mystery about some of the " plant " signs. The Rosebud develops into the Rose. And where there is a Rose there is ever a Thorn. A former landlord of the Oaks in Grays Thurrock became the first landlord of the first inn to open on the new Stifford Clays estate. The child was christened the Acorn.

One of our oldest signs is the Angel, and sometimes inns bearing it are connected with the medieval pilgrims. Occasionally St. Michael armed with sword and shield is represented, but usually the angel is the one who appeared to the Holy Virgin bearing a scroll with the salutation or annunciation. Larwood and Hotten suggest that the Virgin was left out of the sign at the Reformation to tone down the Catholic suggestion. Later, Puritans mutilated the sign still further by blackening out the Virgin as idolatrous, leaving only the lilies. To later generations these flowers had no significance, and it was not long before this symbol of holiness was dubbed the Flower Pot!

Other signs of religious origin are the Golden Fleece and the Crossed Keys. We have already allotted the former to Jason, but it may well be Gideon's. In spite of the Reformation the crosskeys of the papal see and of St. Peter still figure prominently on our signboards. The reason probably lies in the fact that many families incorporated the symbol in their arms, and, of course, many cathedrals—St. Asaph, Exeter, Gloucester, Peterborough and Ripon—are dedicated to the saint.

Mythological signs can sometimes be traced to coats of arms— the Griffin, for example. This beast is represented with its forepart like an eagle and its rear like a lion. A golden griffin is a supporter on the Montague arms. Both chemists and blacksmiths used the phœnix as a sign.

Much guessing has been devoted to solving the riddle of the Green Man. Two of the theories have already been quoted. Two more are given to add to the confusion. A savage clad in green leaves and wielding a club was one of Queen Anne's supporters— heraldically, of course! This figure of Danish origin was borrowed by innkeepers. Again, many morris dancers were clad in green and were thus represented on contemporary signs. When the interest in this medieval sport faded the significance of the signboard figure was forgotten, so he was converted into a green-clad forester. It was but a short step to call him Robin Hood.

Another famous Englishman—by adoption this time—was George, of dragon fame. The saint, with or without the animal, has been a popular subject for centuries. On St. George's Day in the year 1344 the famous order bearing his name was created. Shortly afterwards he was made the patron saint of England.

Adam and Eve have not been naturalized, although they figure on many of our inn signs. They were adopted by the London Fruiterers' Company for its arms. The company was founded as long ago as 1515, and every year in October presents a bowl of English-grown fruit to the Lord Mayor of London.

The phenomenon of the Silent Woman is usually portrayed by a headless female. St. Osyth is claimed as the original. The story goes that when her convent was sacked by the Danes in A.D. 635 she attempted to escape by concealing herself in a thicket, but was discovered and decapitated. Where her head touched the ground a spring gushed forth, and is said to be still flowing. The only inn in Essex to bear this mythological sign was in Widford. But it is no more. So Essex now has no Silent Woman. Alas!

CARVED SIGN·LITTLE BARDFIELD

BIBLIOGRAPHY

A short selection of books which have been most useful to me and will give the reader considerable enjoyment.

Billericay and its High Street	*C.P.R.E. Publication*
Buildings of England	*Pevsner*
Companion into Essex	*Tompkins*
English Inns (illustrated)	*Odhams Press*
English Inn Signs	*Larwood and Hotten*
Essex Countryside	
Essex Review	
Forgotten Thameside	*Morgan*
Historic and Picturesque Inns of Old England	*Hooper*
History of a Little Town	*Walker*
History of Coggeshall	*Beaumont*
Inns of Sport	*Wentworth Day*
Last Stronghold of Sail	*Hervey Benham*
London's Epping Forest	*Brimble*
Old Leigh	*Bride*
The Old Inns of England	*Richardson*
Tales of Old Inns	*Keverne*
The Taverns of Old England	*Maskell*
Trade Signs of Essex	*Christy*
Victoria County History, Essex	